# Interior Realms

Edited by Andrea Cetrulo and Marta Michalowska

# Contents

| | |
|---|---|
| 4 | Introduction |
| 8 | *Secret Places* by Alison Irvine |
| 16 | *Self-Care* by Labeja Kodua Okullu |
| 22 | *Site Report: The Window* by RWP |
| 40 | *Domestic Flights* by Flora Pitrolo |
| 46 | *3 Poems* by Niall Campbell |
| 50 | *The Stone* by Meghana Bisineer & Charlotte Law |
| 60 | *Travelling Home* by Marta Michalowska |
| 64 | *Ensconced* by Stephen Sutcliffe |
| 70 | *Collective Matter, Vertical Life* by Casper Laing Ebbensgaard |
| 78 | *Into the Night (Or Five Rooms at the End of the World)* by Jason Bahbak Mohaghegh |
| 96 | *Manifestos for the Night* by Rut Blees Luxemburg & Casper Laing Ebbensgaard |

| | | |
|---|---|---|
| 114 | *In Praise of Reverie* <br> by Andrea Cetrulo & Victor Ginesta | |
| 122 | *Refuge, Resilience, Residence:* <br> *Queer homemaking for the future* <br> by John Bingham-Hall & Lyall Hakaraia | |
| 134 | *Warmth for the Unhoused, Unfurnished and Uncloseted* <br> by Pol Esteve Castelló | |
| 145 | *Notes on an Image* <br> by Rut Blees Luxemburg | |
| 150 | *Scotopia* <br> by Satu Streatfield | |
| 156 | *Occupying the Shadows* <br> by Andrea Cetrulo & ENDGAME | |
| 162 | *Darker Night* <br> by Michael Salu | |
| 170 | Interior Realms: Audio Compilation | |
| 174 | Contributors | |
| 178 | Endnotes | |

# Introduction

The idea for this collection of new writing across prose and poetry accompanied by a compilation of audio works came about during the public programme *Homemade* presented in partnership between Theatrum Mundi and Agile City from 21 to 23 June 2019 in Glasgow. That programme of discussions, performances, readings and screenings looked at home as a cultural infrastructure. At the time, almost two years ago, and a whole different era ago, domestic space provided a niche infrastructure that was often overlooked in studies examining where culture is produced in cities. Then, working from home was the domain of writers, predominantly women, who cleared spilled milk from the kitchen table and got on with their working day, or bedroom music producers whose commute to the workplace took no more than a split second or artists whose work did not involve dust, dirt, heavy machinery or toxic fumes and who could not either, or both, afford the cost of the studio or justify that expense. Then, in that *long* gone era, most people went out to work daily, while few stayed home. Then, home was a predominantly private space where leisure and chores co-existed, but where essays, poems, novels, films, plays, performances, video works, music compositions, songs, sound art pieces and a myriad of other cultural forms were being produced, out of sight. When we programmed *Homemade,* we wished to draw attention towards creative practitioners making within their homes and the very space of home as an infrastructure underpinning the cultural lives of cities.

    We cannot claim that we had a premonition or magical insight into what was to come. Yet as we started working on the book, which for a long time shared its working title with the Glasgow public programme, the niche infrastructure we wanted to discuss became the central space where employment, self-employment and business activities are carried out alongside all the usual unpaid work of care, cleaning and cooking. Home working became a lived experience of many. Thus, our examination of the domestic space gained a new urgency and broader scope. And here we must add that this way of working is reserved to those who before the pandemic conducted their professional lives predominantly in offices, while those with jobs in retail, hospitality, transport, logistics, food processing, farming, healthcare, care and many other sectors do not have the option to stay at home and still earn a living.

Against the backdrop of this major shift in working practices, we commissioned sixteen new pieces of writing, two interviews and ten audio tracks that we are most delighted to share. We can be reasonably sure that all the contributions are *homemade*, but we feel that, even though the working title *Homemade* was a useful guide and a beacon throughout the process of commissioning and editing, we needed to let go of it as it said little about the *space* from which the commissions come from. In the end, we settled for *Interior Realms*: a domain of reflection, a zone of imagination, a sphere of cosmic reverie, a field of observation, an empire of fleeting thoughts, a territory of contemplation, an expanse that each of the authors and contributors entered to produce the pieces we are sharing in this volume.

The works explore a myriad of themes including nurturing creative practice, self-care, finding grounding through rituals that open space for making work, looking at windows as thresholds, travelling without physical movement, fantasising about living in fictional dwellings from the TV, making music at home that then travels to other homes, escapism and cosmic reverie, being drawn to shape-shifting possibilities of the night in the city, craving the warmth of the dancefloor, and disappearing into interior rooms, corners or the underground of illusion, storytelling and poetics.

We would like to thank all the contributors for their imagination, creativity, generosity, dedication and determination to write and make while confined during lockdown, often in the small hours when children do not have to be schooled or video calls attended. We are grateful to our contributing editors Rut Blees Luxemburg and Casper Laing Ebbensgaard (URBAN NIGHT PROJECT) who drew our attention to the ways in which homes, buildings and cities change with the shifts in the light intensity from day into night, and John

Bingham-Hall who suggested that we should not forget that home does not have to be a domestic space, and that one can find *home* on a dancefloor. Without them our thinking and commissioning would not have been so rich and layered, and perhaps we would not dedicate enough space to looking at shadows, magic, reflections, illusions, pleasure, sensuality and desire.

We hope that you will enjoy the kitchen table, spare bedroom, home office, home studio, garage, shed, bedroom, bathroom, garden, closet and, on one occasion, car productions brought together in this book and audio compilation.

      Andrea Cetrulo and Marta Michalowska
      February 2021

*Secret Places*
by Alison Irvine

These are the people I see when I'm writing in my car: delivery drivers; the postman; boys who run with strong strides; the man who tucks his dog under his arm then puts her down on the grass to pee; the care worker in the Homecare van; the small girl who looks up at the tall man and gesticulates as she talks.

These are the things I hear: doors closing; engines starting; buses; birds; barks; my neighbours talking about firewood.

These are the things I wonder: what is the relationship between the girl and the tall man? (from the way she gesticulates she appears to be an extraordinary girl); who on our street is the care worker visiting?; are the running boys brothers?; would the dog pee before it got to the grass if the man didn't carry her?; aren't all children extraordinary?

Because my laptop has an old battery, I only get an hour and a half to write in the car each time. I take a cup of decaf coffee and a bag of sweets and I sit in the driver's seat, turning on the ignition briefly to wind down the front windows an inch. I put a pillow on my lap, move the seat as far back as it goes, rest my laptop on the pillow and start to write. I don't wrangle over words; I purposefully churn them out and aim for a thousand a day. The car is conducive to that. I like its snugness and proximity to home. I don't take my phone and I can't connect to the wifi.

    I like seeing people walking past. I have my favourites; the man with the pug dog, for example, and the animated child of about five who talks to the tall man. Sometimes my neighbour works in his van while I write in my car. I'm happy to hear the whirr of his drill, but I don't want his eye contact or eyeline. The thought of other neighbours in the second and third floors of the tenements on my street looking down on me makes me self-conscious. But I have no choice. I write in the car. It's a strange time.

I used to tell my children I was going to a secret place. My husband was home. The children were safe and didn't need me.

Once, I saw them leave to walk the dog, a bundle of noise and scooters, a flash of red lead. They didn't see me. Once, when they discovered where I went – they knew, they knew all along – they brought me handwritten notes asking me to watch *Frozen* with them later that day. I wound the window down to receive the notes. *Yes, I will*, I said, then they left me to my work and I returned the window to its place.

I like to lean back in my seat to think, cupping the back of my head with a hand and letting my elbow rest against the side of the car as a driver at traffic lights would. I like the weather on the windscreen: splashes of Glasgow rain or a bright sun exposing black filaments inside the glass.

I read a *Guardian* piece by James Kelman. In the article he talked about writing in his house when his children were young. His kids told their friends to be quiet when they came to the door. They would have learned not to disturb him. I imagine them tiptoeing past his room. I remember staying in the house of a counsellor in Sydney, Australia. *Don't walk past the door when I'm seeing clients*, she told me, the only house rule. *Walk another way.* The house was a bungalow, there were several routes through it, and we walked quietly and stayed hushed while she worked.

Writing in my house shouldn't be any different to seeing therapy clients. But I can't imagine training my children to be so quiet. I find it hard to ignore their petty arguments or demands for help even when my husband is capable of dealing with them. Perhaps I'm a control freak.

A couple of times I lied. I told the kids I was going to the library, said goodbye, asked them to be good, left them to their film, a long film – *Chitty Chitty Bang Bang* or *The Wizard of Oz* – and closed the door to my bedroom. I sat in bed, my husband sat with the kids, and I wrote for the duration of the film. It was surprisingly productive. They didn't think I was home so they didn't look for me. Hiding from and lying to one's children: it gets the writing done.

I also write in the mornings when they're asleep. At times, I've set my alarm at five and worked until seven. I can't do it for long but, if there's a deadline, I must. Or I write when they've gone to bed, but that's more rare. The idea of drinking red wine and hammering the keyboard until one or two in the morning like Hemingway or Bukowski is an appealing one, but I'd be wrecked the next day.

When it's just me in the house, there's always something to stop me from writing. It could be the washing hanging on the drying rail. It might be the dishes in the kitchen that I know are there. It might be the dog or the postman or the landline. It's the internet and all the checks: bank account, jobs, Twitter. It's the skirting boards that need cleaning and it's the thought of the school run at three o'clock. The working day is spent propping up the dam. I remove the washing, tidy the dishes away, pay the bills and make sure there is no clutter in my eyeline. Then I switch tracks to ignore my domesticity and crack on. Music in the background – no words, no spikes, no surprises. There is no choice. This is it. I either write or I don't. The dog watches me from the sofa. She gets up when I go to the toilet. Other than that, she's still. When she was a pup, she used to bark at me and shake cushions in her mouth. At least that's stopped now.

What's best, the house or the car? The house is best for comfort. I get to put a blanket over my knees, make cups of tea or stroke my dog. The car is best for concentration and takes me a bit closer to the real world, because I miss it when I'm writing. That's the thing. As writers we have to remove ourselves from the world in order to write. The car is as close to a creative blank space as I'll ever get. It's my theatre-maker's black box, my room of one's own. But it also has a view.

I wonder about the work that's created within the domestic space that is my house. What comes to light in that twang of tension between house work and creative work? Will that tension show up in my writing? Is that why my prose tends to be sparse and simple? Does it feel a bit taut because that's what I am most of the time? I wonder what it would be like to luxuriate over a sentence or create a Joan Didion style meandering narrative that keeps on returning to ideas and phrases like the folding of flour in a baker's bowl. I'm not a baker. Maybe I just don't write like that. In 2018, I went on a four-week writing residency at Cove Park, an artist centre with a view of Loch Long and the Clyde Estuary. Even with time and beauty and peace, my writing style stayed the same.

I'm still wondering about writing inside that tension in the house. What if your finances are so tight or your circumstances so tough that your house isn't conducive to making art? There's a lot of art that gets aborted. We are missing out on a lot.

My sister-in-law helped me with the writing of my first novel which was based on interviews with residents of Glasgow's Red Road Flats. She grew up close to Red Road. That helped. But it wasn't the main help. The main help was that she looked after my baby daughter while I wrote. I went to her son's bedroom upstairs and she stayed downstairs with my daughter. And that goes on the world over. The minding of children in houses. The enabling of work to be done, often by family members, often by women. She used to bring me cups of tea and pastries called yum-yums. They were. It mattered that I wasn't in my house because my house at that time meant chores and loneliness and tension.

    Those baby days are gone now. I can set my alarm and write at five in the morning. I can write in my pyjamas. I can write in bed. I can drop the kids to school and be working within five minutes of my return.

It's cheapest to write in the house, except in winter, when I worry about heating the whole home for the sake of one person in one room. But maybe that's still cheaper, and certainly more convenient, than a bus fare to the library or two cups of coffee in a cafe, because how long can you sit with one empty coffee cup until you really should buy another drink?

Oughtn't I give to my local economy though? This home working means that the shops and cafes don't get much footfall. This is happening on a bigger scale now: home-working being safer in the pandemic. I like the idea that the coffee shops are around the corner, but that's not enough, is it, the idea of a coffee shop? Perhaps if writers earned more, they could afford more coffees from local shops. I met a woman, once, who said she paid eighty pounds a month for an airy room. If I had a spare eighty pounds a month, I'd do that, and I'd buy a coffee on my way.

I wrote about the Barrowland Ballroom and the Red Road Flats and didn't need a space to write right there. There would've been a room for me, I'm sure, but I chose not to ask for one. The Barrowland was a bit dark and a bit cold when there were few people in it. And it was a bit lonely on the twenty-seventh floor of a tower in the Red Road Flats, so I opted for comfort. And peace of mind. You need that as a writer, don't you? You need that as a human being. I get that, on the whole, in my home.

 I'm wondering what that remove brings to my writing. Wasn't I after authenticity? How could I be authentic writing about the views of Red Road from my basement flat across the city. Shouldn't I have been as close to the Govan dry docks as the boys and girls I wrote about who flirted with crime and delinquency, and whose home lives were only a couple of miles away in distance but so far away from my own, so much trickier and more perilous? Shouldn't I have been in the Barrowland Ballroom suffering its chill air, smelling the beer and feeling what its maintenance man described as the eerie melancholy after a gig when the band and the crew and the punters have dispersed?

 I think about this a lot. The idea of authenticity and the filter that my writing goes through. Is it a bit too snug here at home? Perhaps. It's certainly comfortable sitting propped up in bed with cushions behind my back, but am I too *comfortable*? Is my world view too narrow?

Since having children my world has definitely shrunk. I don't go out much. I've been abroad once in the past ten years. I write within the parameters of my children and that often means writing in the house or the library or the car from which I see the same sights and the same people doing the same things.

I keep Katherine Quarmby's words in mind. In an article she wrote for *The Author* she talks about co-production whereby a writer works with a marginalised community or with people who might not have the agency to tell their own stories. 'During the writing process, I returned after interview to many "former subjects" and talked through key sections with them.' I do that too. I send my interviewees their interview transcripts and say, *This is what I have to work with. If there's anything here you don't want me to use, tell me and I'll delete it.* Quarmby goes on to say: 'But... I also locked myself away to write before delivering my manuscript. I was the author and bore ultimate responsibility.' That chimes for me. I think about this as I'm putting the washing on or cooking the tea. I lock myself away in my house, mostly, or in my car.

I'm lucky to have options: the bed, the sofa, the living room table, the car. I have coffee, sweets, background music to cover up the sound of the laptop's fan, and the sounds of traffic and the rain.

Sitting in my car, in those moments between turning on my laptop and finishing the last of my thousand words, I feel comfortable and inquisitive: *look, I can see those running boys who might be brothers; there's the postman; here comes the care worker; I wonder what the wee girl is saying to the tall man; and, yes, all children are extraordinary.* Something shifts and I find again the impetus to write. Close to home. At home.

*Self-Care*
by Labeja Kodua Okullu

*Caring for myself is not self-indulgence,
it is self-preservation, and that is an act of political warfare.*

– AUDRE LORDE

singing sad songs, walking through St James Park
in the rain, hoping for a dramatic end to the movie
five minute music videos for the coming day
aimee mann/josh tillman/ a deathly comedy
that ends in some acoustic midwest drawl

        take                  1/2/3

        a day in

                          The Life of Irregular Patterns
        everything is fine
        everything ends
                          clean yourself onto a plate
and serve it with hard liquor and youtube
stand up clips/ cooking videos/ author lectures

last night i was so depressed and i went and picked
up Magical Negro by Morgan Parker and if everyone
could, they would really turn around and straighten up,
drunken/sober/depressed/jovial me, we will never lose
so don't worry, don't worry, don't worry

        oh lord, a flower in the desert, is a lonely motherfucker

cocoa butter kisses, talcum powder hugs
fresh laundered towels, lavender scented rugs
my body against yours is my body, my body
against the ground is for the earth, each night
i become a mourning, to wake to the sad news

        I am still a mourning

how do i feel free, how do i fly?
simply walk to my auntie's house
sit in the *mukaase* and *bisa no sɛ*
*aduan bi wɔ hɔ anaa*[*]

---

*mukaase*: kitchen / *bisa no sɛ aduan bi wɔ hɔ anaa*: ask if there is any food

what language do you count in?
i've dreamed in forgotten baby,
toddler debates, that end in sounds
and weakfisted fights, about fantasy
that      real      frightening i defend

sing to me mother, sing to me,
tell me not to play dog games
tell me my food isn't running away
i hear your voice from the corner
of my disorganised wardrobe

      You cry      in pain      only
                        in joy       silence

shout when the need be
my voice is high and urgent
wait for those times to speak
i love the caress of a multitude of song
the buoy of different voices      do not
                                         silence them

      god, please god, a flower in the desert,
      is a lonely motherfucker

can i have a cup of sugar? can i be your wall?
when you fall? will you break the membrane?
my need for what is sweet, shall build you up
my need for more parents shall call upon the
muscles you built in your home with green tea,
shampoo and comfy onesies. my kids would love
to sit by your fire, as you cook for the woman
upstairs who can't get a flat on the ground floor
and can only walk to the shops with the effort
of an olympian, your tupperware magic, your
baskets of essential dreams, i want that power

      a flower in the desert is...

a short film with a woman squeezing a rose till its thorns bled
her dry, in a beautiful garden, she fell drained on a bench,
because she couldn't let go, because she admired the beauty.
how stupid i was to think beauty had to be painful, and that
wonder had to be gripped tight, pulling the life out of itself.
ignoring the lavender bushes in the same garden, to trample
the wild dandelions and miss the sun of the daffodils because
i wanted the rose, its petals full of histories folded inside the
red, like origami stories crafted by a higher being.

    ...it's a lonely motherfucker

who knew sweating was fun? you did, and told me
so now i pour at the least provocation, beard dripping
a waterfall, i dance in it, i dance in it.

shit, me. i caught myself coughing up the rust
of my veins in an effort to soothe my burning
soul, heartrending dramas aren't enough to
tear even my skin, i'm caked in a tar of ketamine,
warehouse shifts and all those house parties

i've seen my friends today and felt myself
floating on the miasma of pizza and beer
the roof sticky with condensed lager and sweat
remotely engaging with conversations
i'll forget on the bus ride home, whilst
they all walk to their houses, settling the body
with the slosh of craft ales, and a warm bed
and their minds turn to health, the cold fingers
of panic, settling on their chest.

        jesus, the flower in the desert, is a lonely motherfucker.

but what to do but save the world?
it's asked of me, i think. it's not too
arrogant to say that i should fix the
world, only if the whole world had
my pride.

and that lonely motherfucker said:

'you cannot touch the earth, till
the tape has played, that squeaking
near warped thing deep within your chest
is furiously blaring in your arteries,
and pooling        deep within your chest,

    screaming   listen   listen   listen

and i told you about tea tree oil, and two litres of water
i told you about running and meditation, i told you about
cognitive behavioural therapy, but bad habits are like a
great song, all you wanna do is hit repeat.

and i told you, no protest before your health, and doesn't
the scent of mint soothe you, so be still and let the world
run rampant whilst your sinuses clear, ready to smell the
stench of burning homes and the foreign scent
of emergency housing, and the whiff of no remains.
the vibrant colours of the lampposts brighten your day

look at me, i dance in the earth, i
grow with the roots of the leaves and i
pray to myself, my body, my pumping heart.
joy is a bachelor, a girl on the town, no time
for the worries of the world, grow your hair
or cut it, or dye it ginger or blue'.

    goddamn, a flower in the desert, is a lonely motherfucker

*Site Report: The Window*
by RWP

I   The Other [half of the] World

On the front cover of Georges Perec's seminal collection of essays *Species of Spaces and Other Pieces* originally published in 1974, Perec peers out at you from behind a set of French windows. He stands with his arms crossed, perhaps because he is outside in the cold or because he feels awkward at having his photograph taken. His face, in contradiction to his body, holds an expression of quizzical mocking, of a schoolboy who has just posed an impossible riddle, a proposition without an answer. Perec is smiling but remote – physically untouchable (on the outside-side of a window) yet his direct eye contact seems intimate and familiar. It is as if he were withholding a secret he desperately wants you to know. This is but one of the photograph's many contradictions.

On that day in 1978, the sky behind Georges has the appearance of a winter fog, a subject he refers to in his short story *The Winter Journey* which looks at the temporal embodiment of poetry's atmospheric space in the physical world. His wondrous halo of frizzy dark hair is both consuming and being consumed by the milky exterior world. The view beyond the apartment window suggests he is on the top floor of the building where the tips of a few bare trees are just about visible, above them a tonal shift suggests a horizon line and a distance that speaks of open space and broad skies. Has Georges left the clutter of his Paris apartment to take up an offer of space and solitude to finish his book? An invitation, maybe, from a friend whose neglected family villa happens to be empty for the winter. While the space of this particular reverie satisfies certain fantasies on the locus for 'serious' writing – expansive (essentially empty) landscapes, monastic interior space, a monochromatic palette – there remains something essentially *odd* about this image.

The top of the photograph (partly obfuscated by the title of the book) reveals railings and a fragment of a window, now everything in this image is suddenly recategorised – the horizon line becomes a tonal shift on the wall of an internal courtyard and the crowns of trees mere light-seeking indoor plants. Technically, the skill required in photographing into the light (through a window) without losing important details in Perec's backlit face or the window frame through which the photograph is taken had to be significant, both in the set up and in the darkroom afterwards. Georges Perec at the time when the image was taken was a consummate exponent of riddles, games and word plays. The ludic literary devices he often employed were instrumental in drawing his readers into playful interactions with his own writing as an active reciprocity between reader and writer. The contradictions in this image prompt questions: was this another of Perec's riddles?; was his intention to ask the reader to enter into the *space* of writing or merely to interrogate what one sees and how one describes what we think we see?

I type the following phrases into my search engine:

Perec front cover of Species of Spaces, a riddle?
visual OuLiPian constraints
shooting into light with stills camera, exposure time?
Maurice Henry / L'Express, photographer, Perec
Maurice Henry, Georges Perec
Les archives de L'Express
1978

Nothing reveals itself – at least nothing that interrogates this image. The identity of the photographer Maurice Henry is attributed to the *L'Express,* the French news magazine. My online searches reveal that Henry, a Parisian resident, was a surrealist poet, photographer, painter and filmmaker who may well have known Perec through the OuLiPi group, a collective of writers and mathematicians who used constrained writing strategies. There is no official evidence of Henry working at the magazine though.

Eventually, I find a small reference in the online archives of the *L'Express.* Following the success of Perec's *Life: A User's Manual* in 1978, the magazine sent the journalist

Michel Bosquet to interview Perec for a feature piece. Bosquet is a pseudonym used by André Gorz – a philosopher, social critic, close friend of Jean-Paul Sartre and idiosyncratic commentator on the French left. Gorz was a significant figure in the student and worker protests in Paris in 1968 and subsequently, following the demise of the movement, became a flag-bearer for the fusion of socialist and ecological politics. As there are no digitised transcripts of this interview, I telephone the *L'Express* archives and speak to Pierre Getzler who sends me a scan of the published interview. Archived with this edition are Gorz's notes in shorthand from the interview with Perec that took place on the same day the photograph was taken. Getzler, now also intrigued by this photograph of Perec, arranges to have the shorthand notes translated into longhand. This piece of documentation has only now been made public and finally sheds some light on the peculiarity of this image.

Maurice Henry (MH) photographing George Perec (GP):

MH    I should like to photograph you in natural light, it won't take long.

[*GP agitated, looks to the window*]

MH    Now... [*moving a desk chair*] if you could sit here next to the window... Don't look so scared, Georges! Relax, enjoy the view, the light is perfectly overcast. Now, as you know, authors are at their best when looking out of a window, as if into the distance, in contemplation of the world outside.

GP    But the world outside this window holds no particular interest for me, Maurice. These authors you speak of... with their 'performing' of contemplation... It's so evidently a confection! Now tell me why I should conform to this inauthentic

charade, for the purpose of 'a good light,'
to make your job easy?

[*Much laughter. MH lights GP's cigarette and slaps him on the shoulder.*]

MH   Georges, Georges... Always questioning, aren't you exhausted?

GP   My friend, it is such orthodoxies that make me exhausted! However, I have endless energy to question the desire for such spectacles... I ask you, will my contrived 'contemplation' sell more copies of the magazine? Back me up here, André!

[*Notes stop here. It is assumed that André Gorz joins the discussion.*]

GP   What did those authors, with their affectations... their silly tobacco pipes, like your friend André, what's his name? [*laughter*] What did they see from their windows? What existential landscape were they contemplating?

MH   A dog taking a shit? [*laughter*]

GP   Aha, indeed, the shit – truly existential, authentic on every level! [*laughter*]

MH   Georges, save your ruminating for the interview. Now sit in the chair and look out that damn window, will you!

GP   Ok, but let me propose something a little different. Why deny the reader this magical vista of contemplation? Why not invite the reader to see what I see when I look out from my window?

MH   But, Georges, this is an author's picture... you have to be bloody in it!

GP  Yes, I will be in it, but I want to be... IN it... the world, where the dog takes the shit, where the air is cold, where the city is loud, in that vista that I never 'contemplate' because I'm too busy writing to look out the damn window! Let this window be my page, Maurice, it will hold me, trap me inside its frame. I will not tilt my fucking chin and look wistfully away. No! I will look into my readers' eyes and I will say, "I am you, I am part of the world too, today it is cold and my view is boring, but here I am in it with you. We are together. The reality of writing is not 'contemplative', it is a deeply... uncomfortable experience."

[*He turns his back to look at the window.*]

I will go outside now and you will take my picture.

Front cover of *Species of Spaces and Other Pieces*, George Perec. Penguin, revised edition 1997.

## II     A Silent [ ] Overlapping

Inside this table, two smoked glass inlays are set in a thick oak frame. The aspiration toward elegance locates it in the 1990s when it was bought in a daze from a vast outlet on the outskirts of town. Its unvarnished underside presses down on thighs uncomfortably, concealing inside its frame yet more leaves of wood and smoked glass. It sits at the window of an empty tenement flat rented to escape the ongoing battle with entropy, where apple cores decay behind cushions, where dinosaurs wait forlorn inside a toilet roll, where the sounds of yelping and outrage prevail.

The horizontal plane makes a mirror out of this table, which holds a singular reflection of the window above. This is a place of silent overlapping. Writing on a mirror makes language a slippage between floating and drowning. The struggle is irrelevant, yet the process of dislocation is pleasurable, like falling when it feels momentarily like flying. Attempts to surface, to hold onto the horizon line, turn the writer's body into a giant eye bobbing up for breath. This eye fixes on unstable vistas: people falling down drunk, a lone man shouting, his chest puffed out and penis exposed, an inside-out umbrella flayed bare on tarmac. At times it's an overheard conversation between two people oblivious to being observed, and the indulgence of a man saying, 'we're fuckin' doomed,' to another while laughing. There are no mouths left anymore, the words spoken on the pavements are hidden behind breath-damp fabric made from old pillowcases.

The table reflects nothing of this street activity, the window chooses only to reflect what it deems important to the writer, namely – the sky, its clouds and birds, fragments of architecture, the crown of a tree.

## III      Therianthropic [ ] Thresholds

The windows are open wide. Their height and width of human dimensions. I stand as if hovering in a doorway waiting to be asked inside.

In Hitchcock's *Vertigo* defenestration happens twice. Illusion and intent haunt these deaths, although in remembering this film, it is only one woman who falls.

Staring outward with a gaze that was later described as 'animal', I observe how the endless roiling of people and creatures below resemble a gruesome grey sea. The breeze, as warm as flesh, unfurls my own body and I watch as it whips and bucks across the city. It flows over the bricks and steel, through the trees and crisp packets and doorways, over gnarled pigeons' feet and sodden baby blue face-masks, through the neglected arcades and abandoned phone booths, past vinegared chip shops and tired kitchen staff smoking down lanes, through the railings being consumed by trees and the buddleia growing from church windows and burnt-out schools, this flesh unfurls past a nervous fox eating pizza and the smell of piss in the doorways, past the river at night and the pungent scent of wild garlic.

My lips are smeared with a bristling grit, teeth dislodge as though my face has been pushed into the remains of something once alive. My body – now a phantom limb – attempts to hold onto this threshold between inside and out, and slowly begins to move back and forth, in and out the open window, hips jutting towards the spires. I fuck the city like this for a while, a slow and languorous brinkmanship between boredom and survival. At climax, I lock with the rising dust arching over the street below, a scream careens out, a sonic awning engulfs the city till, eventually, I'm rasping in a low guttural growl.

I look down at my toes on the window ledge and see they have gnarled into pink pigeon stumps. The skin continues to stretch creating an intense heat. There is an almost unbearable pressure till four black claws burst from the stumps of each foot. A few fat drops of blood hit the street below, releasing a rich ferric petrichor that rises up to meet my salivating mouth. Holding onto the window frame, my balance momentarily tips forward as I try to steady myself while the grounding weight of a tail – full and luxurious – falls softly against my haunches.

I smell a female at a bus stop below menstruating and a carcass of a rat rotting unseen behind the rubbish bins. I look to see if anyone below has witnessed this transformation, my tongue now hanging heavy and happy as I observe the humans below, their heads bent low over their hands. I see they are numb to the vastness I now feel, any urges they possess are mute to the instincts of the feral.

> *Each bird that reaches into my view*
> *with its flight asks for my consent. And I give it.*

I try to pull myself back, to see myself as a human would – a creature framed in a window.

It is then that I become a figment of someone else's mind.

## IV    Without Etymology [ ] Limerence

I think of Baladine Klossowska as I look out from my window. She is most commonly known as mother of the painter Balthus and lover of the poet Rainer Maria Rilke who called her by the pet name *Merline*. Her birth name was Elisabeth Dorothea Spiro, born in Germany to a Jewish family in 1886. She moved to France in pursuit of a career as painter and illustrator, and it was there that she also married, divorced, was a single-parent and lover to Rilke who has since determined her legacy by framing her eternally within a window – his window. Baladine is confined by Rilke within the perpetual state of longing, of sublimation, of limerence – a word without etymology.

In 1924, Rilke produced a small collection of poems titled *The Windows*[1] which reflected on evenings spent with his beloved Merline in quiet conversation looking out from various windows. Baladine (I will use the name she gave herself) illustrated this collection of poems, published a year after Rilke's death in 1927. Baladine's etchings reveal women often contained by a window, as if lost in a trance. One woman fixes her hair, detached from the act; another woman rests with her hands on the windowsill, looking absently off into the distance; another woman (or are they all the same woman?) sprawls naked on a daybed.

When searching for images of these illustrations on the internet, google prompts further associated search terms in the following categories:

> de Rola
> Rainer Maria
> Rilke Balthus
> Pierre Klossowski
> far away
> Elisabeth Dorothea Spiro

> Her son
> Her lover
> Her son
> Her husband
> far away
> Her child self

This is how we are to know Baladine. The [online] window to her frames her so, as seen but never known. She has become the women she illustrates: tranced and somewhat deactivated, yet still performing desirability. Between Rilke's words and Baladine's roaming lines, they are neither inside nor outside, but somewhere between, sealed together – a dead fly trapped in the airless vacuum between the double glazing.

Years later, in 1933, her son Balthus completed a painting titled *Window*. It depicts a woman backed against an open window, one hand braces the sill, the other raised in terror. Against her dark hair is a scarlet headband, her lace-trimmed puff-sleeved blouse has been torn open to reveal a naked breast rigid in the painting's centre. The woman looks upward and to the left of the frame like an image from a pulp novel cover. Behind her, windows in the building opposite look back vacant. They are only a few metres away yet feel distant, abandoned, blank. Her tight skirt, her exposed breast and dainty little shoes, her bare midriff and childish foreshortened hand, she is both sexualised and vulnerable. The window allows us to imagine her impending fall. Balthus, who as a child watched his mother Baladine wait at her window for Rilke to appear, has invoked this aperture and used it, once again to trap and control the narrative of limerence.

Later, the model who posed for the painting reported that Balthus wielded a knife over her while she posed. The long uncomfortable hours holding her position by an open window were frequently interrupted when Balthus saw his model relax enough to adjust her neck or stretch out an arm. It was then that he reached for the knife that lay next to his brushes and raised it high, screaming, *I'm going to rape you, you pathetic little slut.*

## V    [Józef Robakowski's] Eyes

### The Beige Man

is only ever seen carrying a polyethylene bag that is inside out. I call him the beige man as this is the only colour he wears, however, Beige Man has successfully demonstrated that there is indeed a spectrum within the beige colour wheel that is both varied and surprisingly nuanced.

He has a small frame with a slight curvature of the spine, a clean-shaven face the colour of cooked trout flesh and he is balding with a thin line of grey hair above each ear. He walks leaning toward his toes as though on the brink of falling forward. Once I saw him on his front steps talking with his brother and sister-in-law. His brother is a well-respected writer, whose demeanour suggests he is the older sibling. He gesticulates openly when they converse, and I only ever hear the writer speak (he writes in the Glaswegian vernacular). The Beige Man never speaks other than the odd word, but he seems to communicate sufficiently in nods and facial gestures. According to its bulk, his inside-out bag appears to contain small items, maybe a wallet or keys but never groceries, although yesterday he was carrying a bottle of bleach, but the inside-out bag was nowhere to be seen. Perhaps he wanted to disinfect his surfaces – was he expecting a guest? This would be highly unusual, more so now that this is not a government-sanctioned activity.

His curtains have remained unchanged in the fifteen years I have lived opposite. They are a faded rose colour and are consistently neither fully open nor fully closed. I have never seen him look out from his window.

# Four Young Girls

sitting kerbside are all wearing: short shorts, tank tops, white nikes, long hair. They are the sisters who live on Belgrave Terrace. I saw them once in their lobby when guising with my children at Halloween. Each girl sat silent and blood-soaked, holding sweet-filled skulls on their laps: I admired their dedication to character. Now it is summer and they have emerged long-limbed and blanched in the midday sun, each holding a smartphone and using it as a camera to pose for selfies. Their most repeated movements include: hands on hips, tilted jaw, mouth open, hair flicked from one side to another, dipped chin, pouting.

Each movement pivots on the axis of an outstretched arm. The shift from performance to self-scrutiny is disconcertingly abrupt. Following a small discussion, they all prop their devices against a low step, stand back and in unison perform a synchronised routine. On seeing the four phones capture the routine, I lift my own phone to also record this moment.

Score for the Smartphone:

1. Flatten hands like swords.
2. Skim the jaw with a deft slicing motion; elbow leads this movement.
3. Cock head left then right.
4. Toe in, then out.
5. Knees open, knees close.
6. Point both arms down to make the letter 'v.'
7. Fingers at wolf.
8. Retrieve and scrutinise.
9. Scroll. Pause. Finger pinch. Scroll. Pause.

I thumb insta open and post with the words 'street dance'. I see an unseen story ringed in red. It's a poet I follow with rats on her face, her jaw tilted up. She looks good with rats on her face.

walks his dog three times a day. Early in the morning as his dog Sharik (I've heard him call to it) is sniffing along the kerb on the terrace opposite, I watch him stand motionless staring into the thicket of trees and shrubs that separates the terrace from the pavement of main road. The curve of the terrace rises around four meters higher than the main street so that the residential part is separated from the commercial side by a raggedy line of lime trees. I often see men disappear into this threshold of trees and trash to piss, few make any attempt to conceal what they are doing and often emerge with their genitals still exposed. The man decides Sharik has nosed this particular pavement for long enough and begins to pull him away. Sharik refuses to budge and seems stuck on a scent of extreme importance. *That's enough, Sharik!*, the man barks as though giving an order. He is deftly ignored. The man then bends over Sharik, staring with a searching look into his eyes and unexpectedly strokes the dog's head gently. Sharik, grateful for this kindness, rolls onto his back, his pink belly and little tufty penis say, *I'm yours.* The man strokes Sharik along his stomach with his gloved hand, he mumbles softly to him, and they both are lost in this intimacy of soothing and cooing and panting. As the man stands up, Sharik flips on to his paws. *Okay now?*, the man asks. Sharik seems to nod and decisively relinquishes *the extremely important scent* in favour of pleasing his master as they walk on together. With his muzzle raised appealingly, Sharik maintains eye contact with his loved one.[2]

VI    Poem as Window [Frame]:

*Window shopping with Clarice Lispector*

On Avenida Copacabana she is seen, looking into a shop window. The writer José Castello approaches to greet his friend. Later he remembered:

> it takes her a while to turn around
> she doesn't move at first, but then
> before I dare repeat the greeting
> she turns slowly
> as if to see something frightening
>
> and says
> *so it's you.*
>
> At that moment, horrified
> I notice that there is nothing in the shop window
> but undressed mannequins.
> But then my silly horror becomes a conclusion:
> Clarice has a passion for the void.

*Windows at night*, Marisa Privitera Murdoch, 2020

VII   Choreographic Score for a Window
      (A Sigil for the Street)

   [ ] Go to the window with the most light or that
       frames the most external activity

   [ ] Observe this scene from your window.
       Practic shifting focus between what is inside
       and, what is outside.

   [ ] Imagine your window as seen from the outside:
       what is visible, what is not.

1  Detect a rhythm. Select a movement which is not
   a necessity of propulsion.
2  Repeat this movement slowly three times.
3  Remember a time when you waited for someone
   at a window – trace their name in the air.
4  Repeat this air writing till you establish eye contact with
   another person/creature.
5  When eye contact is made, freeze.
6  Try to imagine yourself as that person/creature.

∞

*Domestic Flights*
by Flora Pitrolo

In accepting this invitation to think about the domestic, ambient is the first thing that comes to mind; ambient which is ambiance, landscape. Ambient is a strange kind of music where the landscape comes inside mental and domestic space. After all ambient is so often, but not always, about the outside – the natural world, the environment, all space known and unknown. Cosmic space. It's supposed to make the walls of the tiny flat crumble.

But before it's the space it describes, ambient is what you make it. For me it's Clara Mondshine's *Luna Africana* (1981), recorded in off-time from RIAS, Berlin's American Sector Radio. It's *In the Moon Cage* (1988) by Rex Ilusivii, who used to hand-deliver his tapes anonymously to radio stations in Serbia, and ended up recording in the Amazon before finally dying in Brazil. It's Caroline K's *Now Wait for Last Year* (1987), which takes its sound baton from the metallic corners of the British industrial scene and its electric blue title from a Philip K. Dick novel and fills them with air in the quiet isolation of the hills of Garfagnana in Italy. What you might know or feel about a record is what lands it in an interior space, only laced with spaces of its making. In 1978, Brian Eno took it upon himself in *Music for Airports* to talk about 'an atmosphere, or a surrounding influence: a tint must be as ignorable as it is interesting.' Tint is a useful word. And ignorable, yes: ambient must be ignorable.

Music for the home, music for interiors, 'music for people alone together', music for rooms with no soft furnishings, music for industrial space which *is* a kind of domestic space, and domestic space so irredeemably industrious.

Let's think about ambient as music made at home, to be consumed at home, in solitary confinement. Halting with the teapot halfway – in a strange sense of suspension which nobody witnesses but me and the record. As I write this, I listen to Civilistjävel! – *home-brewed electronics*.

> Music made indoors which doesn't travel much further
> Doesn't need to
> Doesn't want to
> Nobody's watching
> Nobody cares

It's so great that nobody cares. So you can call your first album *Greatest Tits* and you can call your second album *Greatest Shits*, and it's so great that it doesn't need a studio or boys or volume or drummers and, in fact, maybe it doesn't even need people. Let's think about ambient as music for empty spaces. For spaces with objects without us. For spaces with the lights off, when you've finally gone out.

> Domestic exile, home-brewed, homemade, bedroom
> Bedroom label, kitchen label, kitchen sink

But it isn't only the means by which such musics are made, it's the economies of attention they bring with them. The light these things give off. It's the lights these things give off that become an aesthetic. It's the lights these things give off that they call DIY. Self-organised: cheap and intelligent, yes. Luminous and poor, poor and sexy, hibernating but organised. It's the peripheral that feels like the central, the dim that feels glossy on the inside. It's production too *luxurious* to be fazed by the wheels of consumption, on their own merry-go-round. Often lonely, as well as solitary. And it's very boring sometimes staying at home. Very stale, and somehow, very painful. Everything always at the same table…

In the Italian 1980s someone wrote a song that goes like this:

> *the home is without imagination*
> *the home is without wings*
> *the home is a spot of stillness*
> *while life outside blazes by*

And as I type up these lyrics etched into my mind, somehow more records come into mnemonic and aural focus: Max Guld's *For Enden Af Corridoren* (1985), made in an apartment at the end of the corridor on the outskirts of Copenhagen. I've always felt I could see the light of that record coming in underneath the front door of my neighbour's flat at 110 Deptford High Street. *Beep beep.* Now Daniele Ciullini's *Domestic Exile* (1983), made in a room where his father used to design water turbines, which Ciullini had later fitted out with portraits of Lenin, Marx and Che Guevara. *Bang bang.* Now the Belgian band Bene Gesserit comes to mind. They made a record called *In the Living Room* (1981) which is vast and pulsates like a motorway, although it has a heart like a folk song. *Thump, thump.*

Music made inside and kept inside, with the archives under the bed, abandoned in someone's parents' house, in somebody else's house in another city, in another time, by another person whose name after years gets forgotten. Music from another chamber. I spend a lot of my time hunting for this music because I want to hear the music and I want to hear its story. From a recent email conversation with a fifty-five-year-old French artist: *you won't believe the funny things I found in my teenage bedroom.* From a recent text conversation with a fifty-year-old German artist: *I just need space on my hard-drive.* From a recent conversation with a sixty-year-old Italian artist: *Flora my dear, if you find my first divorce papers could you send them back to me?*

> Outsider music is insider music
> Recluse music
> Music made for no reason other than making music

And anyway, who on earth would make music for reasons other than making music? And if you met them, would you accept to have dinner with them?

Sexy art
Political art
Poor art
Arte povera
Cucina povera?

Khrushchev had this category of 'unofficial art', as he called it. He said it expressed 'private psycho-pathological distortions of the public conscience.' The ultimate reason to listen.

Art that had no place in the world *because* it contains all the psycho-pathological distortion of the world is the very art I want to hear. When the windows fly open into the cold night, when the official beckons at the front door, meet me behind the sofa.

And at the same time, it's threatening that home-music tends to travel. The tradition of home-taping runs into the tradition of mail-art: the most personal interaction crafted in personal yet anonymous one-to-one engagement. The collectivity towers over the individual in this particular kind of secret society: from my home to yours, and then to someone else's. There's the dizziness of the network operating on state infrastructure yet hidden from view. Travelling on domestic flights, I imagine an army of glamorous housewives making *musique ménagère*, hijacking the kitchen table into blue international skies. Housework and homework as unnecessary tasks which won't keep the world turning without music to turn to.

On the back of the tapes, you find some addresses from outside the centres of art: outer reaches, outer skirts. Provincial postmen with stories to tell of delivering homemade music beyond the tiny apartment which proves that the network is bigger than the city. Moonshine internationalism. Domestic flights: the world enters the house. Basements and attics, flowerbeds and floorboards, everything suddenly expands like foam.

From living room to living room circulation, distribution, organisation, and in the cracks and sociality of the network some kind of intimacy is to be found: from my quietness to yours, from my isolation to yours. It's even better on the inside than on the outside maybe: time to prepare inside this inwards-looking degeneration, better off alone in the private with an inward-looking public conscience. Nothing good was ever pre-thought, prepared, pre-felt in front of everyone. Never not about the world. Never quiet. Never isolated after all.

Glasgow, June 2019

*3 Poems*
by Niall Campbell

## Tidying While My Son Sleeps

Good luck to us, the blackboard cleaners,
arcing a damp cloth this late at night;
waving off a thin man, his thin house;
the board's returned to quietness,

Nisida, did I get this right?
That nothingness is there and not,
firm, and waiting for a stream,
a face, a woman waving. We work on it,

a little canvas of nothingness,
welcoming the chalk and trace – the boy
asleep, the bed, the room, the house.
Right or wrong, I turn off the light.

# First Nights

Young father, is that you at the night drum,
playing soft, as though the birds were easy woken?
*It's me. I didn't think there was a listener.*

Then why, young father, do you play?
                                        *It snows
beyond the window, the whole house sleeps – and, love,
I'm carrying something that is a change.*

What do you make, young father, of the lateness,
are you a little drunken with the dark?
*Yes, my head swims; I lean this head against
the solid wall, and hum to these new cares.*

So, go on, tell what you hope for, young father.
*Not sleep – not day, not company – just let
snow fall, light burn, glass shatter, let things slide,
let the new change be unlike the old change.*

## Clapping Game

The blue [*] night was on the [*] [*] hill
and my [*] mind was working strangely
after a [*] [*] day of [*] [*] games

and then [*] and then [*] [*] , pouring out
some [*] red wine, and watching [*] [*] as
the [*] [*] moon took its high position,

above the [*] [*] house, seeming like a [*]
stamp of something like [*] [*] happiness,
I reached the point where the clapping stopped

and quiet in the house, night in the garden,
I was free to play that different game;
up late with the world, my small life leapt,
I rolled its dice across the writing desk.

(where [*] represents a clap of the hands)

*The Stone*
by Meghana Bisineer & Charlotte Law

> *A silkworm, with love, builds its own abode by using*
> *its own thread around its own body and dies within it.*
> *We humans wish to possess all things around which*
> *attract our mind. These wants of ours ultimately possess*
> *us and we die for them.*
> [text message from Father, 2:35am Tuesday 6 May 2020]

I started to think of the stone world we inhabit as a prism: in any case it isn't a bubble; bubble is light, stone is solid; bubble is clear, stone is dense. Now, when light refracts through a stone, a solid form that expresses the void, what emanates has the quality of a conscious mind: a conscious mind that is everywhere, perfectly diffused, letting go of so much, and embedded in the middle of your chest bone. I had moved without knowing from the bottom of my neck, your navel, right hipbone down the legs, ankles, feet, toes, wet sandals, and soaked to the bone.

> Quiet nights, a little rip, that silence.
> And then the garden. Which one?

I stepped into my mother's garden in Bangalore, walked to the centre of my grandmother's, with its areca nut trees and me talking to giant snails. Looked around Karen's: it was hot in Oakland and I forgot why I was there. Found some shade in my sister's garden in Cupertino, wait Mysore, and then again in Bangalore: that's how many sisters. London's early mornings in Marta's living-room garden, then long quiet afternoons in Jane's, and, on the roof of your boat, a hot neck, surrounded, moving, green and still. Slow ripples you said, lakes, swimming, waves. And then we did; kiss, eat, sleep, sink like the stone, loved and clear, you breathed in my ear. I felt the weight, light, changing, dancing with its own shadows. A theatre of the unseen: for little people. It's our time.

Did you see me with the feather? I did rise and found myself in my old school grounds lonely in those mundane days that belonged to others, yet somehow comforting. Those inner homes are made of smells and sounds. Swallow, suck, flies. I like your fingers, and more.

We breathed in and were held, like a knot subtly knowing its own strength: I wonder if you could meditate so entwined? My tree became your tree from home, the stone in my hand, the one offered from the beach. Shaped like a fallen angel, its cold weight hinting at bronze. Cast and cast out, still gliding, and okay to be free from all that. Now welcomed and warmed in a hand.

Roots come rushing outwards from the spine. Whitish reaching tunnels hold the body which is at certain points divided: opaque, then empty: lower body, stone; upper body, clear. Like a sun-filled sky, I see a moment or many of your film, the light filtering through my body as if through water. The sun glinting, floating weed and debris, and a heart centred there, like a stone. I love this about the stone; how its way of being changed so fundamentally, moving from an impulse of rejection to considered attention. How it stays with rigour: breathing.

    Breathing in a garden.

Unkempt and wild. I often find myself sitting in a group of remote trees; I see insects, many birds, fragments of flowers. Often blue, all visiting in high definition. Bright, and often so close, too close and too fleeting ever to see a whole. Yet the feather I saw: it was tiny. Soft and gently curled, the size of a thumb nail, it could drift on a breeze for days, dancing around my fingertips but never quite in my hand. We rise, floating, magnetised, blue and green and gold. You're there. We lie together under the stars on the roof of the sea. When the words of the mystic startle me into memory I question myself. What do I want to know? What you saw, and heard, and felt, and thought.

Funny, even though I'd been here before, at the opening I was in darkness. Shifting oval shadows around, intersecting planes of thought form perhaps? I was rolling back a rock within me before my mind could open and soften enough to be entered: once it melts, I can stay, quiet.

I hear a fly. Child.

Take your used-up heart and cast it like a stone, she said, far away and the ripples will soon disappear. I decided instead to hold on to my used-up heart, to my stone, and we like ripples. Dirty glass, hot afternoon, sweaty, sticky tape, tear, stone, breathe, stone. Your voice, small, far away, windy, you said. I held on to my stone and my used-up heart, this was different: is. Is in my body.

I came home a year ago already to you now.

London skies in the river over the Californian bath, the Berlin betrayal, a friendly window, just a bit dusty and the tape like flowers, speedy plants trace the contours of the stone, then it sat in red and stayed. In the midst of so much that was never mine and was always changing, it's your words which stay.

Watching home screening before shuffled tracing paper, a drawn audience of you, crackling across the kitchen table and the walls. Regard: why you're here, and what you're a part of. Would you like to see them in sequence? The darker ones look like eclipses: portals to more than this. Windows, water-stained, reflecting heavy bubbles as they ripple across a cloudy sky.

Think back. The underlying linga* imagines the possibility of a stone with roots; a stone-like a plant with spiralling off-shoots, a stone you can pick up, pop in some water, let live. Inviting a sleepy stretch, a mingling waking awareness of what was already there. As the mind's eye goes in and out of being in the frame of memory, I taste wine from a thermos, hear our quiet *laughter* and the revolving drama of amorous dogs on the run. You tell me of your father. His texts, forwarding, voice, word, image, and translation: time seems less from Bangalore to London.

While I talked of shadows, he talked of peace, while I talked of fears, he talked of work, while I talked of work, he talked of home, while I talked of home, he talked of silkworms, while I talked of love, he talked of mother, and then mid-sentence he passed the phone over to my mother: she talked of boredom, aching bones and a dying body.

> Body like fruit, I said, waking one morning in your boat.

Time stretches vast, when every morning you, my father, write a vachana** in the hand you could not move from your stroke not long ago. When your early mornings meet my sleepless nights, I hold on to every word you say, and we find each other again: like in that photo where I'm in your lap, three years old, me looking up and you looking in. In both times you don't see me, but somewhere in between the vast times and the many homes we find a bit of each other.

> Just like your stone, you said, you who saw as clear as the lake.

It's only when we land distant in the flesh, that together we understand the thinking: the thinking integral to the stone.

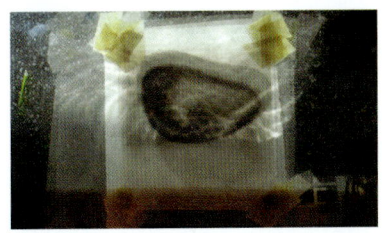

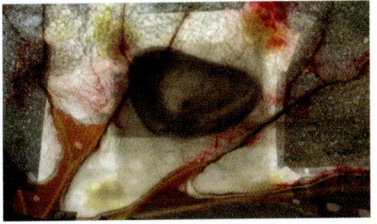

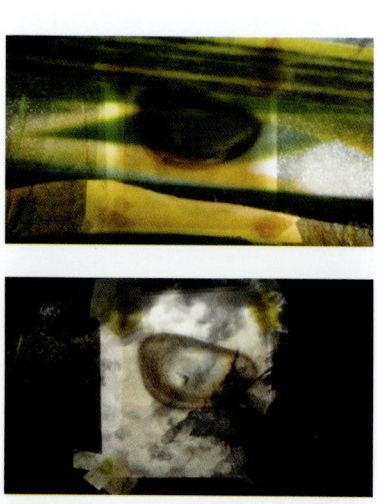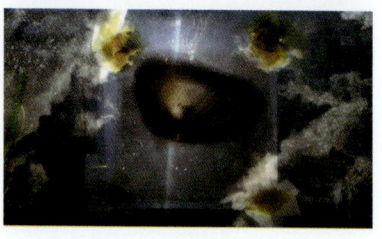

\* LINGA: The Lingayats meditate on a small black shiny stone the colour of indigo/blue black, which is placed in the palm of the hand and raised in line to the eye. The stone is a symbolic representation: a point of attention, or a mirror, to gaze into, in order to return to the self. Every Lingayat has their own Linga, some carry them on their body in special silver cases on a thread, as my parents do. Mine stays at home: an anchor, a blessing. The Stone.

\*\* VACHANA: It has roots in Kannada, a Dravidian language spoken predominantly in Karnataka, South India. The word Vachana literally means 'that which is said'. It is a form of Kannada poetry/ rhythmic writing which flourished in the twelfth century during the revival of 'Lingayatism' (followers called Lingayats; a historical Shaivaite Hindu community) and its secular practices by the movement's leader Basavanna: a Hindu philosopher, poet and social reformer. His movement sought a world without discrimination regarding gender or caste, and leaned towards personal spiritual experience over text-based dogmatism. These teachings were spread through the Vachanas – light poems composed by Basavanna and other mystics. The silkworm text is a Vachana translated and sent via text message as part of my correspondence with my father.

This text results from three writing actions, involving meditation and ritualised reflection upon *The Stone*, the first collaborative film by Meghana Bisineer and Charlotte Law, made over the first few months of lockdown in London in 2020. The images on the preceding pages are stills from the film.

This piece is accompanied by the track *The Stone* by Charlotte Law. See p.172 for more details.

*Travelling Home*
by Marta Michalowska

Her eyes follow a road taking her across a landscape. It's a sunny day on this stretch. She passes a white van with blurred-out number plates. A few clicks further down the road, the skies are grey. They hang heavy over the forest. She feels that her mood is changing. Autumnal melancholia is starting to take seed. But maybe beyond the next bend there will be summer, and the long rays of afternoon sun will shine through dense foliage of birch trees.

She's been up and down this road hundreds of times. Fields, meadows, forests, villages, hamlets, solitary houses, ruins, fleeting signs that are hard to grasp even when she moves only a few millimetres on the trackpad. It isn't a smooth ride towards the horizon. Sometimes she jumps forward in giant leaps. The screen reconfigures and she's missed a whole village. And there is no rear-view mirror. She needs to turn around to look back. And she might find cars that've never passed her while she was moving forward. And it might be winter in the world behind. And perhaps the road has been resurfaced since she's been there a minute or two ago.

She takes a sip of red wine from a stemless glass sitting on her desk next to her pencil holder and a stack of books. She must be over the limit by now. This is her second glass. But it doesn't matter. Still, perhaps she should be careful not to develop a habit of *drink driving,* in case one day she will move across a multi-dimensional landscape, with tyres humming against the tarmac, with vibrations shaking the vehicle as it passes a lorry heading in the opposite direction.

For now, she'll continue her journey around the fringes of Europe, mapping out its boundaries. She tries to stay as close to the edge as she can, moving down country lanes, but sometimes she goes down a coastal motorway cutting through landscape with its four or six lanes. Her vision is focused forward, when she turns her head to look left, there is no sea, her bookcase fills her view. She reads some of the titles: *A Terrible Country, Secondhand Times, Utopia, The Artist's House, Hollow Land, Another Country, Underland, Modern Nature, The View from the Train, Far Country, An Apartment on Uranus, Famished Road, A Small Corner of Hell, East, A Line in the Sand, Hurricane Season, Wild, Imaginary Homelands, Infinite Riches* and *To the Lake.* They might take her somewhere else, each promising a world filling the covers that can be opened at will, but perhaps never entirely closed.

At times, she needs to jump over a sea or a lake. Then, she imagines that she's taken a ferry. She searches for an image of the right water and stares at it as if she were on a deck looking towards the horizon.

She's gone far in the past few months. She's never been quite this far. But she's stayed within the familiar. She didn't feel ready to go to places where her imagination was likely to fail to fill in the peripheral vision. Europe, that was her limit. And she needs to put a disclaimer here. Or perhaps a correction. She didn't dare to venture beyond the borders of the European Union. Although she knows that there is more to Europe. But the exact boundaries are murky. They are a subject to debate and interpretation. There are opinions, arguments and perspectives. And she needs a clear boundary, something solid, established, uncomplicated. It feels that those lines are less likely to blur. She likes to know where she stands.

She gets up from her chair and stretches her legs. She's gone stiff on this long journey. Her left foot is numb from the idleness below the table. The right had its heel planted firmly to the ground, toes hovering above, moving between the accelerator and brake, even if those movements did nothing to the speed at which she's been travelling. She enjoys a bit of speed and would like to let her right foot drop heavily onto the accelerator, making the horizon approach at a breakneck speed, but here speed means a dash forward without any sense of distance passing. It's better to crawl slowly, perhaps not a lot faster than riding a bicycle. But she doesn't like the idea of cycling around Europe, European Union. Too many mountains.

She picks up her empty glass from the desk, walks out of the room, across the hallway and into the kitchen. She refills the glass from an open bottle standing on the counter, takes a sip and turns towards the window. It's gone completely dark.

She hasn't noticed the sun setting today. She doesn't remember noticing it yesterday or the day before. Where she goes, it's always daytime. Mornings blend with afternoons and occasional long summer evenings. The sun never sets. She's never liked driving at night, with not much to see in the headlights, so the perpetual day suits her well.

She's been on the road for a few months now. This was one of those commissions exploring the idea of home, one of those art-in-crisis projects, timely and urgent, and she ticked some of the boxes with her foreign-sounding name, assumed heritage and a track record of writing about place. The deadline has now passed and she hasn't even managed to map out the territory. She told them that the area of exploration was larger than expected and that she needed more time to arrive. They were kind in words, but a deadline is a line, and it shouldn't be crossed. So she's continued on her own, setting herself an alternative one, perhaps more arbitrary than the one they selected, even if it coincides with the end of the year, and without the fee awaiting on arrival. That's fair enough, as she hasn't written a single word. She isn't sure if there will be words when she gets to the end.

In a few weeks, she should return to the UK, crossing into Northern Ireland along the coast of the island of Ireland. She hopes that she'll make it in time. She doesn't know if anything will change on those small country roads other than the speed limit shifting from kilometres into miles.

*Ensconced*
by Stephen Sutcliffe

*Rising Damp*
British sitcom broadcast on ITV from 1974 to 1978

In the 1970s my family's favourite program was *Rising Damp*. It was a sit-com, which took place in a dilapidated boarding house. The regular tenants were a genteel single woman and two students. The main comedy centred round the landlord Rigsby, a lonely bitter throwback who was outwardly repulsed but inwardly jealous of the permissive society. His racism towards Phillip (one of the students), always backfired, however, as this was the 1970s, he was not deprived of a platform to voice his opinions, which today would make the program impossible to produce (although the original is still being broadcast on digital channels).

Alan, a medical student, occupied the best room in the house, which like all the others was a bedsit. It must have been on the top floor, remembering how Rigsby used to charge up and down the stairs to confront him. In the corner, to lighten the grimness (mainly dark Edwardian wallpaper and political posters), Alan's medical skeleton wore a woolly hat.

I have always been able to get ensconced in small spaces. If I have to use a hotel room for more than a few days, it will feel like it is mine. I used to fantasise about living in fictional dwellings from the TV, even before I could understand their context.

*Auf Wiedersehen, Pet*
English comedy-drama broadcast on ITV from 1983 to 1986, then on BBC One from 2002 to 2004

The 'stalag' in this program was the hut the workers slept in. They were British bricklayers, mostly from the North East, rebuilding parts of Germany in the Thatcher era, when work at home was scarce. Other than the hut, I liked the bar they drank in alongside the locals, where they had adopted lager instead of beer.

At the time, I was at the local comprehensive and was more interested in the comedy than the situation. Even though the hut looked smelly, basic, cold and uncomfortable, I wanted my own bunk in it. No doubt I would have soon made it my own. Not with pictures of nude women or photos of the family, but with a nice lamp and a colourful blanket for the bed. Northern humour has always been based in adversity. The idea is to not distract from the situation but to revel in its awkwardness.


*The Man with Two Brains*
American science-fiction comedy film directed by Carl Reiner, released in 1983

I grew up in a semi-detached house built in the 1970s. It was quite modern and, after experimenting with different styles, my parents finally decided on pragmatic decor: neutral-painted walls, tidy furnishings and minimal ornaments. However, my preference has always been for clutter. One year, hoping to receive a CD player for Christmas, my present was a large chair, like the one on *Mastermind*, which I grew to like, particularly for reading in. Then an artist friend gave me paintings and, as the books started to accumulate, my room inadvertently began to look like an Oxford don's study (even though the rest of the furniture was veneer and the curtains and bedspread were printed in a 1980s graphic pattern).

In *The Man with Two Brains*, the mad professor played by David Warner takes Steve Martin to his apartment in a modern block.

'What's the matter?' the professor asks.

'You'll have to forgive me,' says Martin, 'it's just that being here in Austria and meeting a scientist with your interests, I half-expected your laboratory to be in a castle not a condo.'

'You mean like this,' says the professor, opening a non-descript door to indeed reveal a Frankenstein's lair, complete with old stone walls, sparks of electricity and bubbling test tubes.

This was the effect of walking into my room from the rest of the house.


*Blazing Saddles*
American satirical Western black comedy film directed by Mel Brooks, released in 1974

In *Blazing Saddles* Madeline Kahn, as Lili Von Shtupp, greets her visitors, 'Willkommen. Bienvenue. Welcome. C'mon in.' This is ideally how I would like to invite people into my flat.

The downside of working from home as an artist is that you have no 'studio' for curators' visits. Having people round to watch my videos is like asking them over to watch TV. A curator/friend once messaged to say they wanted to bring a group of fifty curators to see me. Panicked, I looked for enough chairs and cups and was about to set off to buy more biscuits, when another email arrived saying that they had meant fifteen not fifty. It was still a tight squeeze to get everyone in. They sat on the arms of chairs and on the floor. The most prestigious curator sat in the best seat, directly in front of the TV, where my works were being shown, and spent the whole time looking out of the window.

*Keep it in the Family*
British sitcom broadcast on ITV from 1980 to 1983

I used to get this program mixed up with one called *Agony* about an agony aunt. In both, the main characters were witty and worked from home. *Keep it in the Family* was about a cartoonist who lived with his wife and grownup daughters in a large suburban house. He had a drawing board in the corner of the living room and wore a lion puppet on his hand when he drew. The joke was that he could blame the bad drawings on the lion.

    I liked the thought of not leaving the house and sending your work away to get paid. His publisher was continually chasing him, because he was constantly distracted. I now have a drawing board in the corner of my front room and my main worries are deadlines.


*Tinker Taylor Soldier Spy*
British seven-part drama spy miniseries broadcast on BBC Two in 1979

I once had two artist friends over and one of them told me that the best advice they had been given was from an old tutor who had said, 'Make everything,' which sounded exhausting.

    I had once accidentally insulted the other friend by describing her flat as 'boho', so to give a chance for *revenge*, I asked what she thought of mine. She said that it reminded her of Inspector Morse's from the detective drama under the same title (1987-2000). I had been going for Smiley's London home in *Tinker Taylor Soldier Spy*.

*Good Year for the Roses*
Music video for the song from album *Almost Blue* by Elvis Costello, released in 1981

Sometimes I daydream that I'm famous and am revisiting the squalor I used to live in before I became successful. Then I come round and realise I never left it.

    At the moment, I am looking for a new place to live. My criterion is that I like that shade of blue light in Elvis Costello's video filmed in a hotel in Inverness. It is the same shade as in a film about William Johnstone making prints to illustrate Edwin Muir's poetry, *I See the Image*, 1981, directed by Steve Clark-Hall. Searching online, I found out that his studio was in a house in the Scottish Borders. The impressionist Rory Bremner and his sculptor wife had bought that house some time ago and had it 'modernised' before selling it and moving back South (another reason to *hate* him). I could never have afforded it anyway. And now I think that perhaps the blue just comes from the time of year, early winter.

*Collective Matter, Vertical Life*
by Casper Laing Ebbensgaard

When walking around the narrow, densely populated streets of interwar Naples, Walter Benjamin noted how life teemed across its multi-storey buildings, bestowing upon the city a vital sense of disorder. Windows, balconies, doorways, rooftops and stairwells provided the 'popular stage' on which the 'animated theatres' of everyday life played out.[1] In recognising the cultural significance of these *domestic* sites to the formation of an urban *public*, Benjamin suggested that Naples had more in common with the African *kraal* than it had with Northern European cities, insofar that 'the most private affairs' were conducted in communal settings as 'a collective matter'.[2] And, nowhere was this more evident than at night.

Benjamin was drawn to the convention-defying practices of Neapolitans and notably the children who played in streets way past midnight, catching up on sleep instead the following day, napping behind shop-counters or in stairwells. Sleep was not sacrosanct, confined to the shaded secrecy of the bedroom; there was no fixed 'hour, often no place, for sleeping';[3] rest was instead something they would 'snatch in the shady corners'[4] of the city. In Benjamin's Naples, intimate life was not restricted to the private sphere, but constituted a publicly shared sentiment that evidently collapsed conventional boundaries between the home and the city, work and play, interior and exterior life.

The vertical layering of public displays of intimacy suggests that at night people's homes emerge as mundane sites of cultural production. But how do people who occupy these glowing private spaces – that so often are aestheticised in cultural representations and writings about the city – experience their participation in this public production? And how do their home making practices provoke radical rethinking of the ways in which intimacy is sought, forged and wrought in the public night?

In my ongoing research, I have been seeking answers to these questions through spending time with residents of high-rises in east London, visiting them and walking with them at night, exploring how they have built connections to the human and more-than-human worlds they inhabit at night. Most of them have been forced to reinvent their ties, as they moved into or became neighbours to one of the 200 towers more than twenty-storeys high that have been built over the past decade, and which precede the onrush of another 525 towers planned across the city. In London, as in any vertical city, the intensity of proximate life leaves its residents exposed and open to their surroundings; the architectural preference for glass has seen windows merge into walls, merge into façades, merge into skins. Life becomes translucent, just like in Benjamin's Naples. To Raahil and Aishah, a couple I met in their two-bedroom flat on the twentieth floor in a recently completed tower in Aldgate, east London, this kind of translucency is measured with equal amounts of despair and hope. Their sense of *home* is weaved through continuous negotiation of the city's intrusions in ways that forge supportive infrastructures in their everyday lives. In thinking about the home as a site of cultural production in the vertical night, Raahil and Aishah brought my attention to the often mundane, if not overseen, domestic patterns and routines that are established in continuous negotiation with their immediate surroundings.

Sewing Light

Raahil remembers his mum working out of their home when he was a child. People would drop by with clothes for her to fix and come back to collect them a couple of days later. The sewing machine was placed in the bedroom he shared with his brother. It was the only place that they could make space for it. When Raahil and his brother went to bed at night, he remembers falling asleep to the soft thuds of the machine as the dim light gleaming from the lamp carved out a silhouette of his mum hunched over the needle. The glow slowly shifted to each of her miniscule movements, and Raahil recalls waking up and falling asleep again to that dim flicker.

When Raahil turns off the lights in his flat at night, he can see the entire city before him. There is so much glass in their living room that the light from the buildings and streets around streams in through the windows and fills the space. Their flat is not at eye level with the street, it is twenty storeys above it, so streetlamps and shop lights do not shine directly in. The city lights are just intense enough, as if they have been filtered on their travels from the street, for Raahil and Aishah to feel a sense of connection to the glimmering buzz of moving vehicles and people in the streets. The preinstalled ceiling lamps that hang in each corner of their open plan kitchen and living room are almost futile. They are too bright, Raahil and Aishah told me, so they prefer to light a few candles instead to complement the city's glow. They leave the TV on or open the fridge or the built-in cupboard in the corner of the room if they want more light, letting incidental sources stream into their living space.

Dimming or completely turning off their lights allows Raahil and Aishah to see the city beyond, lets the outside enter their flat and become part of their home, while too much light produces reflections in the glass and cancels out the view. Keeping the lights dim complements the bright lights that burn in the city night, not in the sense that it replicates them, but that it compensates for their glare, evens out the score, balances the light levels to provide a balance in their lives. They enjoy spending evenings in the dark, looking out at the city as it changes at night, as its lights flicker, some turning on, others off, reminding them of the otherworldly excess that burns into the night.


Floors One-To-Four

When you enter their lift and brace yourself for the minute-long wait in vertical transit, there is nothing of real note. The elevator itself is fairly dark, lulling its passengers into a mute doze. But as soon as the doors slide open, a burst of intense brightness burns itself onto your retina. Rather than stepping into a residential corridor, it feels like being in a hospital or a doctor's surgery ready for an operation. The brash lighting that, under the pretence of safety and security, has become a much-debated marker of social difference in the UK reigns free in Aldgate. Building code dictates that corridors have to be kept bright at all times, but here they exceed the requirements threefold.

Raahil and Aishah told me that they only became aware of how bright their corridor is, when on occasion the elevator stopped on one of the floors one-to-four. There, heavy mahogany front doors that sit deep within dark wooden frames glisten softly in muted, warm light. Those corridors lead to privately owned flats and their residents have fobs that allow them to manipulate the elevator into a halt on those floors. To Raahil, Aishah, and anyone else living on floors five-to-twenty-one, these buttons do not exist. They can press them all they like but the lift won't budge.

While the brightness of their corridor never fades, their dislike of it has. They have grown quite fond of its refreshing shine. As an antidote to the numbing dullness of the lift, their sparkling corridor embraces them on arrival before letting them transition into their dim-lit home. The stinging glare feels almost celestial to them.

Sky

When Raahil first set foot in the flat, he couldn't believe the view. Having lived all his life in a maisonette on a council estate in Bethnal Green, surrounded by towers, he had never been on the twentieth floor before. He had never seen anything like it. The agent who showed him around the flat, told him that this one had the best view in the block: unobstructed sightlines towards the City of London and the Olympic Park in Stratford.

When Raahil sits down and looks out of their windows, he still feels that overpowering sense of immensity that captured him so forcefully on his first visit. If you bend your knees a little and look out the windows, all you see is the sky. A friend who recently came to visit him after work, lay down on his sofa and turned towards the windows and just stared out through them in complete silence. When Raahil asked what he was looking at, his friend responded, 'The sky.' 'And the planes,' he added later.

When you are this high up, all you see is the sky and the occasional plane or helicopter flying past. Perched above the chaotic streets and just below the flight paths, Raahil and Aishah are held in an almost noiseless vortex, a translucent air-space insulated from the markers of Modernity, but always firmly attached to the hollow lift shafts that make verticality possible. The vast expanse of the sky pulls Raahil and Aishah out of their domestic confines, providing a bit of space in their home and in their minds. The alternating effect between enormity and interiority has long preoccupied psychologists and psychoanalysts who often invoke the spatial analogy of buildings and rooms to explain the function of the human psyche. With reference to our ability to dream, to draw and to write of the world that surrounds us – spaces in the past and those we imagine in the future – Gaston Bachelard suggests that the spatial and temporal immensity of the world never exist as something distant, detached from the body, 'out there' and away.[5] Instead, these 'elsewheres', however fragmented or distant, are brought into being by our ability to populate them with our bodies and inhabit them with our thoughts. What he termed 'intimate immensity', describes an expanded notion of being that repositions the body as a conduit through which distant times and spaces flow. The presence of the sky in Raahil and Aishah's home, draws them out of their immediate space and offers a version of intimate life that is constituted through the elements they live *in* and the things they dwell *among*.

Closer

Raahil and Aishah told me that they pray five times a day. The first prayer is at sunrise, which in mid-summer is about 4 or 4.30am. Getting up at this time is an incredible experience because the city is completely different. Raahil can see the head- and taillights of cars in the streets below, but there is almost no noise. When he opens the windows the air is cooler, making the city feel cleaner, fresher. Raahil has heard that the higher up you are, the pollution gets lighter.

When they pray, they bow down and touch their foreheads on the prayer mats they have spread out on their bedroom floor, lowering themselves to the 'ground level'. Even though they are on the twentieth floor, dropping their bodies like that allows them to ground themselves in the space and find inner peace. The position of the body is important, they always face the sun that rises behind the cluster of towers on Canary Wharf, which on clear mornings will refract the deep-red rays of light bursting through the stack. The aim, Raahil explained, is not so much to shut out disturbing elements or suppress things that cause worry – this isn't Mindfulness or other kinds of Western Buddhism – but rather, to focus his mind and body on connecting with the 'natural' elements. Since God created the sky, the sun, the clouds and the rain, Raahil and Aishah feel closer to the Creator when they are perched in the sky. It is not their elevation that makes it easier to 'reach' God – they are just as capable to pray in their local Mosque on Whitechapel Road – but the total immersion in God's creations – sky, clouds, mist and light – makes them feel closer to their Creator.

Translucence

The ordinary theatrics that Benjamin noted along his nightly strolls in Naples were so captivating because they exceeded the formalism associated with domesticity. This drama, Benjamin suggested, offered glimpses of odd imaginaries and partial fantasies that revealed another kind of city which belonged to the realm of fiction rather than 'reality'. Of course, the two cities constantly coalesce, sometimes in subtle and at other times in quite violent ways, but always to produce new meanings and openings. Life in the vertical city is translucent, insofar that the terrains between the physical and metaphysical shift, and open up for different ways of being. For Raahil and Aishah, their windows, stairwell, lifts and balcony draw the elements they live in closer to their lives, and sustain their religious, recreational and more mundane routines. The translucence of vertical living undoes the distinctions between the skin of the body and that of the building, unsettling the idea of a home as interiority; in the vertical city, the home is, as in Benjamin's Naples, always a collective matter.

*Into the Night*
*(Or Five Rooms at the End of the World)*
by Jason Bahbak Mohaghegh

There are those nights of rare existence when certain rooms open to us, rooms of a more deranged intimacy where we can tempt the last boundary of experience: to disappear forever. Thus the art of disappearance begins from the construction of an interior space – a single room, corner, underground – where we bisect ourselves into two opposing figures: the trespasser and the nemesis. Function of the trespasser: to steal power from this temporary domain. Function of the nemesis: to dissolve whoever enters into thin air. And it is Night that stages this contest; it is in nocturnal hours alone that we seek the hiding-place that turns us toward hiddenness itself (the forgotten, the incognito): these last rooms of the earth, built to suit the last nights of being, though their remoteness transpires right within our midst.

We will therefore follow a sequence of five world authors of Night, glancing quickly at their conceptual configurations while also noting the three unique domains of spatial enclosure in each display of storytelling and poetics.

This piece is accompanied by five audio tracks by Jason Bahbak Mohaghegh and William Messenger. See p.172 for more details.

# I     FIRST NIGHT (of the purgatorial future)
*Interior Spaces: the Bedroom; the Screen; the City*

> Everything, finally, unfolded in a place resembling a deep, inaccessible fissure. Such places open secret entries into darkness in the interval between midnight and the time the sky grows light. None of our principles has any effect there. No one can predict when or where such abysses will swallow people, or when or where they will spit them out (...) The deepest darkness of the night has now passed. But is this actually true?
>
> —HARUKI MURAKAMI[1]

The First Night suspends us in the aerial camera view of a futuristic city, the setting of Haruki Murakami's *After Dark*, where Night itself plays the main character, guiding a strange plot of barely-intersecting events and figures between the hours of 11.00 pm and 4.00 am. However, scattered throughout this textual universe of urban contours and nocturnal meetings are short interludes that take us into the heart of a lone bedchamber: it is something like a bare hotel room located somewhere in the badlands of a metropolis; the lights have been turned off and a young woman rests in a deep unnatural sleep upon a single mattress, her slumber being the work of some unknown diabolical force, and across from her motionless body a television flickers with the live video feed of yet another empty room; at its centre, an ominously masked man sits on a chair. He is watching her intensely and pulling her gradually through the screen to the other side of the virtual. Thus we are confronted with a disturbing tension: we must bear semi-omniscient witness to Night as the site of abduction, and yet we are not allowed to interfere (all are purgatorially stranded).

*The Bedroom*: It is the workshop of technological sorcery, a minor island amid the infinity of crisscrossing districts, alleys, and all-night clubs beyond its four white walls. This bedroom is also where we readers are converted into insomniac voyeurs while she remains hostage to absolute somnolescence: we cannot speak to her nor influence

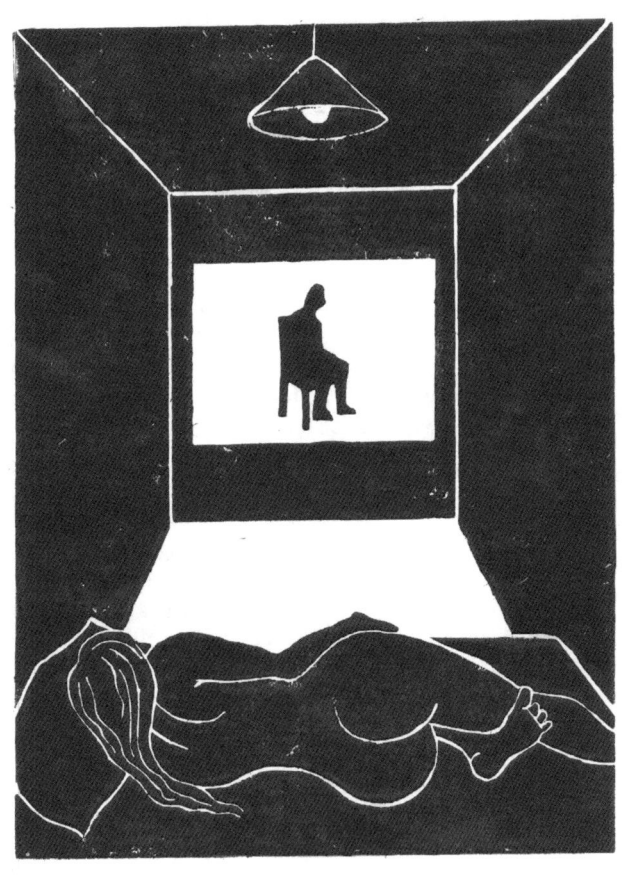

the procession of events, but rather must observe at close distance this reverse-divination system where gods move backwards (from emergence to vanishing).

*The Screen*: It is the separating curtain that functions both as barrier and portal between the so-called real and those zones of utopian reproduction, digital recording, and immortal circulation through which once-palpable beings become floating images. The screen thereby reconciles the ancient problematic of the inside and the outside by serving us this new riddle: we must first insulate ourselves in order to abandon the world (sinking into palest abstraction), like those many fairy tales tried to instruct us long ago, each filled with immersive adventures (into the forest, the closet, the well or rabbit-hole) that always led to some soul-stealing affair.

*The City*: It is the ultimate diversion – its grand spectacle of noise, artificial light, and consumptive excess are all just distractive particles meant to conceal the alchemical work of this one room (...) where a resting sacrifice finds herself pulled through chasms of eventual absorption. Before dawn, she will become permanently entrapped in the blank static of the simulated; she will lose herself to the evening of the machine, the invention, and the faceless intelligence that wants our human throne. Thus the after-dark streets teach us another crucial paradox about this futuristic concept of Night: sometimes the most impersonal spheres are required (the modern cityscape) to execute the most personal violence (existential theft).

II     SECOND NIGHT (of the ancient ritual)
       *Interior Spaces: the Library; the Labyrinth; the Ruin*

> Throughout the course of the generations
> men constructed the night.
> At first she was blindness;
> thorns raking bare feet,
> fear of wolves.
> We shall never know who forged the word
> for the interval of shadow
> dividing the two twilights;
> we shall never know in what age it came to mean
> the starry hours.
> Others created the myth.
>
> —JORGE LUIS BORGES[2]

The Second Night allows a certain time-travel across the frontiers of imagined antiquities, for which the later hours operate as windows into an exotic pseudo-history: their spatiality is that of the unbound figment; their temporality is that of the never-transpired past. And so it is that Jorge Luis Borges rises to the occasion of his own prophecy above (to 'create the myth') by slipping actual names/facts of eclipsed civilisations and elapsed eras beneath the layers of his own fictive projections and embellishments. Such is the ultimate gesture of shadow-play: to fantasise archaic twilights, all the while himself slowly going blind (toward perpetual nightfall). And so it is that we detect three recurring interior realms situated throughout his short stories – the library, the labyrinth, and the ruin – each of which takes on dynamic silhouettes and cryptic morphologies when handed over to those ancient nights that had never happened. In "The Library of Babel", rogue seekers come from far and wide to search the endless shelves by candlelight, each looking for that skeleton-key answer that will fulfil all questions (though going perplexed by its futility). In "The House of Asterion", a lonely Minotaur recounts his tragic fall from royal bloodlines into the demented architecture of the maze, where he endures a destiny of wandering, solitude, and beastly cruelty (until surrendering himself to a death-drive). In "Circular Ruins",

a mystic returns to a jungle clearing filled with sacred debris where he dreams a young boy from nothingness – testing the fringes of perception and materiality by willing him piece by piece, organ by organ (the pulsating heart, the skeleton, the eyelids) into moulded incarnation, only ultimately to realise that he himself is the apparition of some other magi's speculative flames. All three stories take place in ancient nights; all three are full of ritualistic turns that reveal fate as something shape-shifting, enigmatic, or deviously obscure.

*The Library*: It is the great seducer of mind and curiosity – sages, elders, and seers traverse its columns and sift through its endless pages; they carry torches to illuminate its ever-stretching aisles and hunch their backs lugging heavy volumes from table to table, never realising that this desired Night of the one true word is in fact the Night of the lost cause. For this Library is the abyss of the illegible: they enter as readers; they take their last breath as readers still. It is where interpretation goes to die, at the outer edges of exasperation; it is where thought perishes by sheer geometry.

*The Labyrinth*: It is where we meet the isolated one – half-man, half-bull – whose miraculous hybridity is devalued into an object of stigma and sadistic gamesmanship. He boasts of his noble lineage; he boasts of his minimalist tastes (not a single piece of furniture), and how he has mastered the elaborate circularities of his home. He tells us that he often splits himself into two identities in order to gain company, chasing himself around corridors or flinging himself masochistically from heights until his curved horns and heaving animal torso are left covered in blood. Nevertheless, none of these sad descriptions of long solitary nights can conceal the fact that people scream in horror at the mere sight of him, and that he devours nine men every nine years by command of a mad king who marvels as he feeds. So it is that the labyrinth is where we discover the radical torment of the perfect killing-machine.

*The Ruin*: It is where otherworldly projects are escorted carefully into the world, as visionary elders lay tables for their rites of astonishment, metamorphosis, and manifestation.

He kisses the dust beneath him before entering into vertigo; he hallucinates the formation of arteries and veins that give rise to a child's physiology; he mouths certain spells silently and sways below the full moon. Later, he teaches the child the secrets of the fire cult and its singular delirium. Thus the Ruin is where forbidden appearances become flesh and bone, as the tears of a crying mystic give rise to the most intricate practices of conjuration, and thereby tying Night back to those etherealities that walk and breathe among us.

### III THIRD NIGHT (of totalitarian dystopia)
*Interior Spaces: the Warehouse; the Hallway; the Cell*

> What happened then? I don't remember. Lost in the night of time. (smiles) But he wasn't so innocent.
> —GRISELDA GAMBARO[3]

The Third Night begins by malevolent invitation: we arrive at an aristocrat's gated estate in the middle of the woods (resembling a vampire castle) or at a metallic warehouse (resembling an industrial storage facility). Such is the setting for the macabre political play of Griselda Gambaro's *Information for Foreigners*, where we ticket-holding visitors are given specific passwords and clear regimented guidelines that are nevertheless coated in arbitrariness, for they are employed simply as levers of domination and exclusion. This place is where those literally 'disappeared' are held, an entire generation of alleged rebels wrested from their homes in the middle of the Night and subjected to procedures of extraction, coercion, and erasure. A guide appears at the door's threshold to divide us into groups and take us on a tour of this place of torture and untimely executions: its architecture unfolds in sinuous trajectories, gallery upon gallery, like a haunted house or the freakshow of an ill-sitting carnival (for all is obscenity here).

*The Warehouse*: It stands like a fortress or citadel of grave proportions, announcing the symbolic authority of some regime (the overlords) who nevertheless enjoy playing out their sickly pleasure-principles in a sort of decadent theatre. This reveals to us what we have always intuitively known (from fables of the emperor's clothes): the state is nothing more than a ceremonial production, a conspiracy of emblems and choreographed visual tricks meant to induce paralysing awe/control (society as magical prison).

*The Hallway*: It is what consolidates this grand dungeon into a series of micro-passages, all filled with the dank air of suspicion, as we experience the vice-like tightening of space around us (claustrophobic immensity). It is the triumph of a profane fractal unity, one through which brutal vertical hierarchies are somehow scattered horizontally in grim episodic arrangements. Still, the hallway also allows us a kind of criminal fluidity, a route in-between entrance and exit from each scene of forced confession, electrocution, or hanging; it reinforces our feeling of parasitic gazing and complicity all the while rushing us to the next crypto-tunnel before any trace of shame can enter our collective consciousness. For its narrowness guarantees our anonymity in the shaded background.

*The Cell*: It is the dead-end of being, the juncture of impasse and confinement. This is where we observe the disappearance itself, a glance into the inner sanctum where those banished from everyday life have been deposited and reminded of their extreme vulnerability. Some of the guards are lascivious in their interactions (mockery), some are cold as ice (assassination), some are emotionally reckless (rage), some are surgically precise (tyrannical rationality), but all occupy this last station of the cell with the same intent of imposing punishing immobility (nothing can be done). Thus the cell retains the solemn quality of those antechambers of the early pyramids and temples, their walls painted with iconographic journeys of the dead, though no longer reserved for pharaohs and queens (exaltation) but only for the enemy (hatred). So it is that Night belongs both to the forces of totalitarian structures and their revolutionary saboteurs.

IV    FOURTH NIGHT (of schizophrenic encounter)
*Interior Spaces: the Garden; the Drawing; the Asylum*

> One night in the sixth year of her life a dream takes her
> behind the tall mirror which hangs in a mahogany frame
> on the wall of her room (...) She enters and finds herself
> before a staircase which she climbs. She does not encounter
> anyone. She stops in front of a table. On the table is a small
> white card (...) Then her vision appears to her for the first
> time: The Man of Jasmine! Boundless consolation! Sighing
> with relief, she sits down opposite him and studies him. He
> is paralysed! What good fortune. He will never leave his seat
> in the garden where the jasmine even blossoms in winter.
>
> —UNICA ZURN[4]

The Fourth Night occurs in a temporal-imaginative crucible (the night's dream of daybreak) through which children and madwomen are brought together in an exercise of immanent pretending. So it is that Unica Zurn's *The Man of Jasmine* recounts the tale of her supposed marriage to a chimerical figure when just six years old, an extraordinary meeting in a grove that sends convulsions over the next decades of her life, from her surrealistic visual art to recurring psychotic collapses, drug experiments, and periods spent in and out of insane asylums. His vague presence inspires her to become increasingly obsessed with numerology (particularly the number 9) and to start devising compulsive anagrams (poems where the letters are rearranged to form other words and coded messages). And her drawings depict backdrops of wild enchanted spaces: gardens, thickets, endless vines and plants intertwined, and strange vegetal beings with many eyes and faces among them. The ideal kingdom for the Man of Jasmine. Thus she sketches the Night of a lunatic infatuation over and again.

*The Garden*: It is where the first trembling emits itself, the first oath sworn, both of them blameless in their promise and exchange of subtle vows. Moreover, the garden is no bygone memory: it is the prime altar of the word 'yes', embodied in her lifelong attraction to snakes and serpents

(she sees them everywhere), and hence a site of hypnotic delight and eternal wish-making.

*The Drawing*: It is where she protectively encapsulates her gentle oneiric world, holding the Man of Jasmine's profile in the simplicity of lines, amid methodologies of schizophrenic layering, amid journal parchments and canvases full of entangled trees that give refuge to his half-entrancing, half-frightening look. Thus the drawing is the space of the soft touch and the safe haven.

*The Asylum*: It is the last place she spots him, amid the barrage of electro-shock therapies, white robes, sedatives, and false caretakers. It is not long after that she becomes a nocturnal martyr, throwing herself from an apartment window while on short leave from the asylum, thereby fusing Night to the troubled love of the phantom and the phantasmatic.

## V     FIFTH NIGHT (of the idol's revenge)
*Interior Spaces: the Land; the Case; the Museum*

> In a glass room
> In a museum that squats
> in a lost city that crouches
> in a deserted land
> on a vast continent
> I live, elevated, confronting the eyes of men,
> and paralyzing them.
> At silence's end, I shake off
> the events of time, and the
> terror of the ninth century.
>
> Idol of Nineveh
> Its Master.
> (...)
> In terror, tribes of the dead
> make me blood offerings.
> How many voices
> tremble with the nightmare in the cadence
> of the chant
> I was called many names
>
> —MAHMOUD AL-BURAIKAN[5]

The Fifth Night sits us across from an object of adoration and catastrophe (the idol), an artifact of pagan tribes from ages of plague and legend, whose chilling form combines features of the alien, the animal, and the monster. This is the focus of Mahmoud al-Buraikan's poem "Tale of the Assyrian Statue", told from the perceptual vantage of the icon itself, force of both atrocity and survival, reward and curse, neither pure fiend nor pure saviour, in whose chiselled body we sense some lurking bad sentience. Yes, we must tread back thousands of years to when those first civilisations worshipped graven images that looked nothing like human beings, far before the monotheistic-anthropomorphic reduction to a metaphysics of sameness, to the so-called savage intuition about reality itself: the universe does not resemble us, and thus its creators must also proceed from different motives, desires, instincts, tastes, and wonderments. This is what the ancestors thought of the apparent chaos that ruled their nights and of the puppet-masters manipulating circumstances of fatal consequence (floods, storms, fires, war, famine), such that all the

gravity of the cosmos could be possessed in this one small thing called the idol. [Note: Does this meditation on indeterminate nights bear noting that the poem's author himself was stabbed to death one evening at home in old age by a roving band of looters?]

*The Land*: This is where the local idol first circumscribed its dominion, over a particular stretch of borders that marked its definitive territoriality: it belonged to only one geo-circle, its name was recited by only one people's chant, into which it poured its vital thirst and powers of rejuvenation. We can imagine the incantatory songs composed in its honour, and we can imagine the ruthless night-raids carried out beneath its stare, for the origin of any land is also coterminous with the logic of potential invasion, exile, treason, and conquest.

*The Case*: This is where we find the old idol held in the contemporary timescape of the poem, in a state of translucent containment behind some glass of an exhibition that offends its own prized materiality of gold, silver, bronze, rock, or marble. The case is therefore a device of humiliation (it casts into irrelevance), antithesis of the pedestal. Nevertheless, the longer we linger before the idol's peering eyes, the more we are intimidated by the creeping thought that this glass cannot hold it forever, and that perhaps it still holds enough animistic energy to crash outward and escape one night.

*The Museum*: This is the great modern carceral from which our entity patiently plots its revenge (angry return). The majority of the poem's verses revolve around tales of its endurance and the many centuries of insult it has suffered – the miniature figure tells of its glorious jewels and rings being stolen by caravans of thieves, of being buried beneath desert sands, of being mishandled by children, ants, and wolves, and of the hammer-marks and gaping holes now strewn across its once-smooth form. The museum is therefore the space of final grievance; its monumentality is testament to its guilty share in assuming the precursor's obsolescence, though it is from whose basements the idol will again unleash its Night of long-awaited resurgence and reckoning.

‡ EPILOGUE
*Five nights; Fifteen interior realms.*

Nocturnal experience never gives rise to identical patterns: rather, its time-space opens onto a limitless hall of mirrors in which one can find all conceivable remnants and possibilities (including strands of ecstasy, captivation, fear, mystery, evil, passion, and abuse). It houses all the phobias and manias of our race, and others, our masks and invocations, playing host to whatever superstitions or rumours entertain us at a given moment.

In our epoch alone, there are countless treatments on such reflective prisms of Night:

...psychoanalysts like Gaston Bachelard have sought 'those dreams of extreme night' where 'the dreamer will find no guarantee of his existence.'[6]

...philosophers like Maurice Blanchot have asked, 'Is it at Midnight that "the dice must be cast?" But midnight is precisely the hour that does not strike until after the dice are thrown, the hour which has never yet come, which never comes, the pure, ungraspable future, the hour eternally past.'[7]

...poets like Alejandra Pizarnik suggest that 'Night is shaped like a wolf's scream' and that 'those eyes were the entrance to the temple, for me, a wanderer who loves and dies – I would've sung until merging with the night, until dissolving naked at the opening of time.'[8]

...and avant-gardists like Roger Gilbert-Lecomte describe dim-lit scenarios where 'a woman dozes on the roof her name is night / Ancient abandoned to the perils of intoxication / To sleep's fumbling treasons... / The name is night she sleeps with one eye open / And all the world at stake on what she sees.'[9]

No doubt, all have carved out their own special recess of the after-dark; all chase its puzzles and sub-compartmental illusions as if the whole world depends upon it (and they are right). For Night is simply the name we give to the unravelling, to the rise and fall of all things.

*Manifestos for the Night*
by Rut Blees Luxemburg & Casper Laing Ebbensgaard

Night has always been a space of alterity and resistance to the conventions and hierarchies of day. Darkness encourages a different mode of perception, perhaps more reflective, more immersive, more durational. That is why you not only see differently at night but think differently. Know differently. We want to suggest that *nocturnal perception* opens up the possibility of a distinct form of *nocturnal cognition*. The spectrum of a *nocturnal knowledge* is more curious, more permissive, more associative, and because it is more risk-taking, it opens up and questions hierarchical orders that saturate the day.

Darkness allows for different alliances and interactions.

Rut Blees Luxemburg, *Londonium*, 2019

*Londonium* is confusingly ambiguous. It recalls the Latin *Londinium*, the Empire before the Empire. But it is something else too. Something in-between. The *Tudor* font emphasises this temporal in-betweeness, it confuses times, aesthetics and signs, creating a fertile confusion where other meanings emerge, where you look again, where you associate and improvise with possible meanings to come. Another time, another sign.

*Londonium* sits in a vertical hierarchy of signs. It is above the INA STAR Hair & Beauty Salon, i.e. the body. It is above the shutters, above the walkways, above the street, and the stone. It is an aspiration. But not just that.

*Londonium* deals with immigration. Litigation and family business. With personal injuries. And landlords. These are serious matters that need attending. Today, more than ever.

Rut Blees Luxemburg, *Icarus Project*, 2016

As darkness falls, the daytime city shuts down. Hoardings are firmed up, shutters are rolled down, doors locked up, windows closed tight. The boundaries are reinforced in a attempt to prevent leakage, to avoid the unruly night to seep through the fissures of its maintained surface.

Those cold, metal barriers for keeping out, away and at bay, become enticing surfaces of potential pleasure and excitement. Their unintended excess that flows and bleeds goes beyond strict utility. The gold rush that revels behind those protective barriers of private development and investment lures towards secret passages, providing the inverted maps for your own Eldorado. In the *Icarus Project* sodium glow turns everything to gold.

Rut Blees Luxemburg, *The Retreat*, 2005

At night, the fractured and partial visibility frees your perceptive registers from *seeing everything*, it draws attention towards the soft, ghostly glow that stands out as if it were carved out in the dark, with alluring qualities that have the capacity to draw you nearer and pull you closer.

This is not, of course, only an urban phenomenon. It is not only cities that seduce by light – just think of moths or Greek mythology where the attraction to light, the sun and the stars reveal its elemental allure. The shine and shimmer of reflected light playing on a façade, on a surface of things, has a deeper elemental quality, like the piercing sun that plays in the ripples of the sea. The spectral glow that emerges from endless refractions and deflections of light in a bent neon has a captivating effect, like the haze of the setting sun.

Light is fired by combustive processes. Both flames and diodes flicker with life. It doesn't make sense to talk about natural or artificial. From *Londinium* to *Londonium* it is all cyber-luminous. The expansive night sky is cyber-luminous, the towering cranes are cyber-luminous, the cosmic constellations are cyber-luminous. Astronomers and night revellers might have more in common than they would have thought.

Rut Blees Luxemburg, *Caliban Towers II*, 1997

Hackney Council had an inspired phase in the 1960s of naming their housing estates and towers after Shakespearean characters. Situating the present moment in history, making the historical present. While the recent naming of residential high-rise buildings is meant to engender the aspirational economies associated with height, conquest and ascent – The Pinnacle, Principal Tower, Altitude, Landmark, or The Halo – the ambitious period of welfare expansion drew on the high-culture through the characters from Shakespeare's comedies and tragedies. But this seemingly innocuous practice had an unsettling charge when a building was named after a fictional villain.

For the fourteen-storey tower, forming part of the Arden Estate in Hackney, the council chose Caliban – the rebellious and 'monstrous' inhabitant of a far-off island in *The Tempest*. With Prospero, a proto-type coloniser, arriving on the island, Caliban was forced into slavery, accused of rape and tortured with dark, harmful magic. Caliban is an anagram of the Spanish word *Canibal* used derogatively to characterise Carib people during settler colonial times.

Shakespeare's Caliban was mortified when he saw his own reflection. In the 1990s, Caliban Tower was surrounded by barbed wire and prominent security cameras which imposed on the wider estate a panoptical system of control and observation. In *Caliban Towers II* the curtain of golden leaves sets the towers on a stage. The luminous crown softens the frame and allows the towers to emerge through their anterior glow, re-imagining the urban night.

Rut Blees Luxemburg, *London Dust*, 2013

The cyber-luminous night appears throughout the city in crystalline form, glinting in our eyes. Cyber crystals are reminders that the mediation of 'reality'– analogue, chemical, mechanical or digital – has never been manipulation. Not even distortion. But always construction.

When the construction of The Pinnacle – the tallest building to crown the cluster of sinister-playfully named towers in the City of London – began, CGI images announced the future skyline on the hoarding around the site. A visual insemination, a silhouette adorned with an architectural Helter Skelter. Ironically, its alias, The Helter Skelter, served as the perfect analogy for the confusing flurry that forced the construction to a dramatic halt. The financial crash of 2008 left the aspirational dreams of an architectural Tivoli hanging in mid-air, on the twelfth floor that had been completed out of the proposed seventy-two. While the developers pulled out and scrapped the project, Kohn Pedersen Fox's design lived on in the streets. The awkward presence of a future never realised became part of post-crisis living.

*London Dust* is an urban trajectory. A reckoning with life among ruins and a realisation that eventually everything returns to dust. From *Londinium* to *Londonium*, all succumbs to slow and steady decay that haunts dusty streets. Pollution, oxidation and dereliction are reminders that just like buildings and structures they will return to the pits from which their construction materials had once been mined.

Rut Blees Luxemburg, *Vertiginous Exhilaration*, 1995

When you find yourself among cyber-luminous clouds, hanging somewhere above the streets that teem with life, it is difficult to dispel the economies of aspiration which invested so heavily in heights. Rising above the city, mesmerised by the journey through the building's core, captivated by the elevation from floor to floor, you are lured into a promise of gaining *more*.

But when you experience true *Vertiginous Exhilaration*, you are pulled out of the world you nominally inhabit. Seeing it anew, not with clarity or foresight, but through an absinth-green sulphur-haze. Hallucinatory heights followed by a come-down. You are reminded that like the tower you too are attached to the ground, and that no matter where you stand, you occupy land. At least, in *that* moment.

The thrilling experience of *Vertiginous Exhilaration* is not an escape from the world but a return to it. Just like love is something we *fall* into, the vertigo is a way of falling into the world, or being thrown into it. If the cyber crystals you encounter in *Londonium* provide you with an inverted map of hidden passages that lead to Eldorado, *Vertiginous Exhilaration* is the push and pull of liberation made possible by being thrown into the urban night.

*In Praise of Reverie*
by Andrea Cetrulo & Victor Ginesta

What to do when your world suddenly turns upside down? While the economic, social and human impact of Covid-19 is yet to be fully quantified, it is already clear that the pandemic has ravaged the cultural sector: shows and festivals have been suspended, concert venues have shut down, and theatres and cinemas are being swallowed by mounting bills, while their incomes dwindled. The successive confinements, enforced quarantines and scores of preventive measures have further destabilised what was already a precarious environment for those working within the arts and culture, and artists in particular. In this situation, one may be inclined to get subsumed in sadness and melancholy, but it is also plausible to appeal to introspection and reverie to subvert difficult circumstances.

Etymologically, the word *reverie* comes from the Old French *resverie*, meaning 'wild conduct, frolic' or even 'raving, delirium', and *resver*, 'to dream, wander, rave', and it was not until the sixteenth century that the word gained its current customary meaning, which translates into 'a state of thinking about pleasant things, almost as though you are daydreaming'. According to the French essayist Michel Montaigne, it is an 'activité de l'esprit qui médite, qui réfléchit'[1] (an activity of the mind that ponders and reflects) or 'pensée obsédante' (obsessive thought).[2] *Cosmic reverie*, as conceived by philosopher Gaston Bachelard, is a phenomenon of solitude whose sole entry requirement is to have a pretext. In this state, introspection takes over family drama, solitude takes over socialisation, and situates one in 'a world', not in 'a society' of contracts, transactions and conventions.[3] Yet solitude, the cosmic reverie's inseparable companion, often carries negative connotations, especially when voluntarily chosen. The renunciation of a civic persona in favour of a more reclusive lifestyle raises the question whether an individual is 'productive' and contributes to society while temporarily disconnected from some of its dynamics. Patrick Leigh Fermor relativises this assumption after spending long seasons among cenobitic monks: 'What good do [monks] do, immured in monasteries far from all contact with the world? (...) No more than any other human beings who lead a good life, make (for they support themselves) no economic demands on the community, harm no one and respect their neighbours.'[4]

The extrication from worldly demands does not necessarily derive from a pure self-serving banishing of the world but rather a suspension of it. As Albert Hirschman argues in *Shifting Involvements* (1982), civic life and the implication of a public persona in social change may not be linear, following instead the logic of a pendulum, shifting from periods where public participation is in the limelight to moments where private goals and aspirations take centre stage. This dynamic may be useful to understand artistic processes, which may require periods of reverie to nourish creativity and to make room for new ideas.

A Room for Reverie

A home can become analogous with physical and psychic interior spaces as reflected in Charles Baudelaire's poem "The Double Room", an ode to solitary *cosmic reverie*: 'A room that is like a reverie; a room truly spiritual, where the stagnant atmosphere is lightly touched with rose and blue.'[5] Similarly, in the satirical essay "Philosophy of Furniture" (1840) and the gothic short stories "The Tell-Tale Heart" (1843) and "The Fall of the House of Usher" (1839), Edgar Allan Poe's decadent descriptions of claustrophobic architectural settings and domestic furnishings transform every room into a literal *living room*: an architecture of interior, anatomical space englobing a nightmarish world.[6] The realm of the domestic can also become the place where to entertain escapism and access other possible worlds, as in Clarice Lispector's short story "Love",[7] where the protagonist, Ana, defamiliarises her everyday domestic surroundings through reverie, temporarily exiting her ordinary life as a bourgeois housewife in Sao Paulo.

Yet all these rooms are permeable to the exterior; domestic reverie is porous, an interim: Ana returns to her responsibilities after daydreaming detours, retreating back to the home, the shell. So does Baudelaire, whose sublime encounter with the otherworldly in "The Double Room" is interrupted by a 'heavy and terrible knocking [that] reverberates upon the door (...) as in a hellish dream'. Ushers, a concubine and an editor torment him with trivialities and reminders of the pragmatics of life, distancing him from his trance.

Reverie, in its most radical incarnations, begs for a complete disconnection (even if temporary) from a public persona and life. Des Esseintes, the main and sole character of J.K. Huysmans' novel *À Rebours* (1884), epitomises this separation: an aesthete who refutes realism in art and retreats to a house on the outskirts of Paris where he recreates an alternative universe filled with eccentric paraphernalia (a 'mouth organ' from which he 'drinks sounds'; self-made, artificial flowers; a gem encrusted turtle; monastic furnishing in one of the rooms) that allow him to experience the world on his own terms. The epigraph to the novel, borrowed from a thirteenth century Flemish mystic, illustrates the overarching sentiment: 'I must rejoice beyond the bounds of time... though the world may shudder at my joy, and in its coarseness know not what I mean.'

Although self-imposed isolation has its genesis in religious ascetic traditions, the quest for expression through individualism in Western art gained traction with Romanticism and the Decadent movement. In "Solitude", Baudelaire wrote an apology for self-absorption:

> A philanthropic journalist once said to me that solitude is harmful to man (...)
>
> I do not demand of my journalist the courageous virtues of Robinson Crusoe, but I ask that he not summon in accusation lovers of solitude and mystery.[8]

He proceeds by invoking Blaise Pascal who wrote that 'All of humanity's problems stem from man's inability to sit quietly in a room alone.' A century after Baudelaire, the maestro of cinematic desolation, Andrei Tarkovsky, would encourage youngsters to learn to enjoy spending time on their own from an early age to liberate themselves from the anxiety and boredom that might emerge from their inability to do so.[9]

Isolationism

Beyond its romantic connotations, isolation has proven beneficial to many artists as a way of nourishing creativity, cementing the liaison between retreat and artistic creation. But what kinds of hermitism emerge from within contemporary cities as a product of their intense alienation, and how do they affect artistic creation? Richard Sennett offers one perspective in *The Fall of Public Man*:

> In privacy we seek out not a principle but a reflection of what our psyches are, what is authentic in our feelings (...). Each person's self has become his principal burden; to know oneself has become an end, instead of a means through which one knows the world.[10]

Although this points towards an accentuation of narcissistic attitudes in modern cities, the benefits that introspection may have for artistic creation as a way of escaping urban distress (everyday social pressures from the media and artistic milieus, the struggle for survival, and so on) are also significant.

As such, daydreaming and urban alienation are a koiné in current Western music. Both are often projected in songs, may it be through escapism or self-absorption. The former is for instance captured in Burial's post-rave *saudade* track *Night Bus* (2005), where London's cocktail of fog, rain and cold, tinged with melancholy and despair, can be felt in the bones. In this track, reverie is as claustrophobic as it is sentimental: scintillating daydreaming and the drama of loneliness. The latter is obsessive, reverberating with urban seclusion, and paradigmatically incarnated in a current born on the fringes of rock, techno and ambient, named *isolationism* by journalist and musician K. Martin in 1994:

> Isolationists asocial music is providing a suitable ambience for those people placing their faith in solipsism (...) this isolationist strain uses the studio as a monastic retreat to encourage self-confrontation.[11]

According to the Oxford Dictionary,[12] being isolated means 'not near other things or people of the same kind', and the word comes from the Latin word *insulatus*, meaning 'made into an island', and later from Italian *isolato*, with its root *isola* meaning 'island'. Therefore, its most direct translation is being stranded on an island, like Karin, the troubled character played by Ingrid Bergman in Rossellini's *Stromboli* (1950). Given its meaning and etymological origin, it is hardly surprising that the images evoked by isolationist music are located in the wilderness, and while the music remains rooted in Brian Eno's consideration of ambient music as environmental music to decorate spaces, its sounds deal with dark chords, textures and atmospheres that seem to be an expression of unease and discomfort.

'My music becomes fully connected to my retirement from external life',[13] explains isolationist German composer Thomas Köner, whose works from the 1990s onwards take inspiration from glacial spaces. In spite of isolationism being eminently an urban music, some of the most emblematic releases project a dark riffing around insulation, retreat and natural phenomena fetishism. For instance, their covers refer to natural elements: the snowy mountains of Biosphere's *Substrata*; the minerals of Lull's *Cold Summer;* the stalactites on the compilation *Ambient 4: Isolationism*; and the mouldy, seemingly underwater, vision of Scorn's *Gyral*. Song titles such as Lull's *Lonely Shelter* or Main's *Crater Scar* further reinforce the association between getting *lost* in nature and getting *lost* in urban disengagement. This connection is made via a sonic *retreat-through-reverie* that resembles a modern incarnation of the romantic escapism from city to forest. The feeling of seclusion is not uncommon in modern urban music, largely made by *bedroom producers* working within the context where the room is at once the studio, the shelter and the prison. Thus, the home-studio becomes the space from where to experience new altered and distress-informed states of reverie.

## A Child of Extremes

As these examples show, reverie can be a dynamic force for artistic creation, adopt a myriad of forms, and be the reflection of a manifold of mental states and underlying motivations. It can be an exercise in self-knowledge through introspection, contesting conventional notions of productivity, and enabling creators to distance themselves from whatever was disturbing them, be it anguish, overstimulation or social pressure, and at the same time allowing them to focus and create.

In times of social crisis (as the one we are living as we are writing this), retreat from the pace of external demands and public narratives of current events may be a relief, and even a blessing in disguise, for those artists whose home is at once a shelter and a refuge. Poe, Baudelaire, Lispector and Huysmans exemplify the ways in which architectural interior spaces mirror spiritual interiority and vice versa, and the ways in which a home can be a host for introspection, the development of the *inner eye*, reverie and imagination. Although reverie starts from the individual, and is primarily for itself (an exercise either of self-care or self-destruction), it speaks *about* the world *to* the world. Modern urban experience suggests not only the strong interwovenness of creation, precarity and alienation in cities, but also the potential power reverie and retreat may sometimes have to overcome the jolts of life. However, as the eighteenth-century commentator Antoine de Rivarol suggested, 'to lose oneself in reverie, one must be either very happy, or very unhappy. Reverie is the child of extremes.' As such, reverie may be a dear animal to love or an untamed beast to fear.

*Refuge, Resilience, Residence:*
*Queer homemaking for the future*
Interview with Lyall Hakaraia
by John Bingham-Hall

VFD (Vogue Fabrics Dalston) is the only independently QTIPOC (Queer, Transgender and Intersex People of Colour) owned venue in London that operates as a not-for-profit company. It is a Community Arts Venue supporting marginalised artists, groups and collectives who have common intersectional interests.

I remember clearly the first time I heard of VFD. Late one night in Dalston, having stumbled out of Dalston Superstore (back when it was the only place open past midnight on Kingsland Road), I heard a voice: 'I know a place.' I don't remember who said it, but I wanted the night to continue, so I followed a loose group through the dark, empty street, and found myself descending into a basement at 66 Stoke Newington Road. It was more like arriving at a house party than a nightclub, with Lyall as the effervescent host. It must have been two in the morning.

VFD became my regular late night, the place I could go out to without arranging to meet anyone, but still be among friends. I later ended up living in a shared flat a few doors down, just after finishing my Master's. I ran into Lyall in the street one day (the first time I'd seen him in sunlight) dropping their daughter at a dance class. We got talking: I was waiting for a job to start, they asked me if I'd like to do some shifts behind the bar. I ended up working there for much longer than I needed the job, right into my doctoral studies. VFD was a home for an expression of myself that was less evident in the company of my academic colleagues: working as dwelling, alongside an occasional, nocturnal family of queer people of colour, trans folk, and party boys, who served drinks, cleaned toilets, and hung coats together.

I wanted to speak to Lyall for this book because VFD seemed more like a queer home to me than any other nightlife space I've known, but also because it is their home, an experiment in vertical and temporal diversity of use.

JBH   Tell us, who is Lyall Hakaraia?

LH   Rangatira Takatapui Toi (Queer Arts Director). As a Pacific Islander we are a Pluralist and our pronouns represent the many – We, Our, Us, Them, They. An artist and designer who has a built a community through an arts space that celebrates, embraces and supports 'Otherness' in all its diverse forms. We are an expert in creating work with progressive artists in the face of adversity. Our recent work looks at combining community and performance in the making of ritual. Lyall is a founding member of Faggamuffin Block Party and Inter Island, the first Pacific arts collective in Europe.

JBH   There are multiple forms of home, or homeliness, or domesticity, that exist at different levels of the building that you occupy. I'd like to ask you to talk about what you understand those to be, what forms of home you can see in your building.

LH   It's a home for me, and my daughter. And we've got a cat, two birds, and three fish, and lots of pot plants, and a couple of dogs. It's a shelter for us. But then, it's also a shelter and a home for people who come and stay with us. These are people who are facing abuse in its many forms: whether their own personal abuse of drugs and alcohol, or people who are being discriminated against. So my home is a refuge. And then, the downstairs is a venue – a *home* to very different groups of people. It started out as a focal point and a centre for the queer community in Dalston when it first opened, because there wasn't any other space like it. These days it's much more a music and performance space, especially for queer people of colour and femmes. It's changed with the shift in narratives around queerdom and the changes to Dalston itself.

There is also my studio where we make things: clothes and props for different productions and photoshoots. The studio is a home for me.

There's a lot going on in the building, but it all follows what I see as being of interest, or needing help. And obviously, things keep on changing, naturally. Circumstances change. Society changes. The people you work with change. So, it is an ever-changing, ever-evolving, many-layered version of a home, a house, a safe place.

There're so many words that are being used for home at the moment, especially in queer communities, especially for people who don't have, or maybe aren't able to go back to, a home, for various reasons. Or people who seek to find a new family.

JBH  I have a sense that there's something about the way queer people find family and commonality in nightlife that makes clubs and venues become temporary homes, even if just for a night. But of course, for some people, coming into nightlife spaces might not feel like home at all. I'm wondering if you could think about the different ways the club space has been used. Or how have people found refuge within it?

LH　　We haven't been that prescriptive about how the space is used. It's been everything from a performance space to a photographic studio, to a dance space, to a workshop area. We very much leave it up to organisers to fill or create their own home. Sometimes people only come here once or twice. Acceptance is what is really important: knowing that whatever people come dressed as, whatever their gender is, whatever their sexuality is, they'll be welcomed and won't be questioned. I think that's super important for people.

JBH　　I've seen people come and really feel a sense of ownership over the space, which is something that the bigger clubs in Central London probably can't offer. And I guess this must have a lot to do with the fact that it's also your home and you have the leeway to offer people the invitation to make themselves at home. But at the same time, there must be times when tensions emerge?

LH　　For lots of those bigger clubs, it's all about the bottom dollar and making money. That has obviously been somewhere in the background of my business model, but not particularly at the front of it. Another thing with bigger clubs is that they are well-known brands. You are a hot, sweaty man, with his top off, dancing up and down, and you become the image of what that club is about: a clone. Whereas with Vogue Fabrics, when people put out imagery of what their night might be about, or who they're hoping to attract, I want to see four or five very different people that attend your club. It can't be the same thing over and over again.

There's a risk in that though, of diluting the audience. In lots of ways, it's good to have a strong image: 'we want people who wear heels, have bad wigs, and wonky makeup, and that's all we want'. There is an audience for that, and you could cater just for them. That said, I've never seen our space as being colonised by one particular group. If we silo... That fabulous word. If we siloed ourselves to just one thing, then I think we'd ruin something about being queer as well.

JBH     So creating a *chosen* family, something that feels extremely comfortable, where everyone is sharing something clear like bad wigs and wonky makeup, could have a danger to it. It almost takes on some of the constraints that the traditional family has.

LH     Exactly. And if you're not doing that, then why are you here? For me, now it seems much more important to create space for those people who are most marginalised: black trans people or young trans or nonbinary kids. They are most in need of *home* or the idea of home. And I can't see it getting any better quickly, unfortunately. I've got better at programming, and looking at, and understanding that more, I think.

JBH     Maybe we could talk further about the normative version of a family and the notion that constructs it: sharing a house. That's something you gather around, where you moderate your differences – gender, age, etc. And, of course, many people within families are not biologically related.

LH  Certainly. It's really hard to celebrate oneself, when you've got nothing to celebrate against. Those differences you are talking about are very much present at VFD, among the groups that call it home. We have always had a super mix of age, ethnicity, definitely gender, and sexuality as well, and that's why things are much more dynamic. This enables you to last a lot longer, while places that have a certain look or a certain way of being become *tourist destinations* within the queerverse. I think diversity is so important, and the idea of family and home is always about that diversity. If all the children were of the same age growing up, or everybody was the same age in a house, it wouldn't work.

JBH  To make a parallel with cities, when a city relies too much on one economic activity, and that stops working, then the whole thing collapses. You need a whole ecosystem of different approaches, different cultures, different ways of making culture within the queer community.

LH  Absolutely.

JBH  With the club being closed during the current pandemic, I imagine you're able to keep going because you also have the studio within the building?

LH  I've always worked for myself. It's been thirty years now that I've been making clothes, but having other interests has always been important. While I was running fashion labels, I started making clothes for performers, and doing magazine work including high-profile ones such as Vogue: French, Italian, and British. I think part of the reason for starting the venue is that it seemed like a natural progression from dressing superstars, going on tour with them, or going to their gigs. And I had the space downstairs from the studio where I could do it. I would never have entertained the idea of having a club if I hadn't been working with different performers at the time, producing some of their shows, going on tour or helping with sets.

I think I was also still working on Glastonbury quite regularly then as well. There was a crew that came back from the fields in the winter, still wanted to go out, and get drunk, and have some fun. I was having parties through the whole house. And then I realised. Instead of having people invading my home, let's make a space where people can come and maybe not destroy as much of my house. So, it changed.

When we first opened, everything was begged, borrowed, or stolen. The curtains were black silk from Swarovski. My friend used to hang their chandeliers for all the big shows all over the world and he had that black silk that became the curtains, which then, of course, everybody started to have sex behind.

JBH    I remember.

LH    The benches were from Arcola Theatre. We just took them. I still have no idea whether they were left out to be taken away, or if we just got lucky. And our DJ booth, the first one was an old 1950s glass cabinet, which we found in the street next door to us. So, it was quite DIY the way we created the space.

JBH  Exactly. I used to do the door sometimes, or the cloakroom, which spills into the studio when it gets too full. It always felt like the materials and the whole atmosphere of the studio seeped into the club. Often, I wasn't sure if things were made for the club, and then it ended up in the studio, or vice versa, like daytime and night-time worlds overlapping.

LH  With the big jobs in the studio, where there might be ten of us working on one piece of clothing, you have to give everybody a sense of purpose and a sense of being part of a family, otherwise things just don't work and don't get made on time. With the club, there has to be some vitality to it, some mystery or myth making going on around it, for people to want to come, and fashion is all about that. So I transpose the skills I've learnt in fashion onto it. You're alluding to something else continuously, and this keeps people interested and keeps them coming back.

JBH  I really like that phrase 'alluding to', because in the dark of the basement, where nothing's quite clear, everything is an illusion, and also an allusion.

LH  You give people a few clues and let them fill everything else in. There's always that dot, dot, dot. You have a hundred people at a party and each goes home with slightly different stories of what happened. As long as there's that excitement in the air, people will want to come back. Love Art Magic: that's what I am practising.

JBH  Love is at the heart of the domestic, art at the studio, and magic at the club, but they must all spill across all parts of the building?

LH  Exactly. Absolutely. And that's the thing with living upstairs. Most of the time, I'm very happy to have the space to myself, or just me and my daughter, but I think there are times when it's good to have other people. I went through a phase of going out and meeting people, and thinking, oh my God, you're going to be a superstar, you just need this little [finger snap] to get you going. Why don't you come and live with me for three months? You don't have to pay any rent, but you do have to be out in three months. And I can introduce you to people, we can help you find somewhere to live, and get going with it.

JBH  It sounds like an artist residency: a space to refine creativity, and then go back into the world. So for you, the domestic is not fully private. Your own domestic space becomes a public resource, to some extent.

LH  There've been lots of occasions when artists wanted to perform here – Christeene or Mykki Blanco, for example. They'd come and stay for maybe one or two weeks. You're playing a host.

I think it's a slightly different role to nurturing, as on tour, where the performers more or less have their shit together. They've managed to make an album, they're out of their own home countries, and they're doing it. They've got a certain amount of chutzpah to do that already. Whereas sometimes when I have people staying here, they are more of unknown quantities.

So, I am... I wouldn't say weary, because I'm still doing it, but you have to be aware of what you're taking on. All those people bring different elements into your life that otherwise you just wouldn't have.

JBH  What you're doing is such a dense use of a building: a residency space, a refuge, your domestic space, a making space for fashion, and a club that takes so many different forms.

LH  The idea of home and family is going to continue to change, especially with resources becoming more and more precious, and the changing climate. Those spaces that bring things together are going to become more and more valuable for everybody.

JBH  Maybe queerness can be thought of as a way of countering narratives of efficiency and sustainability that are just about reduction. Sharing as a strategy.

LH  Exactly. Whatever the future will be, it's going to be a mess, so we must get ready for it. I'm interested in creating new, resilient queer communities and queer spaces for the future. What I mean by being resilient is being able to absorb and respond to change, not just to cope.

　　The advantage of being queer is that you see the world in a completely different way. It's a gift, and people have to see it this way. There are so many alternative solutions to every problem. We need to rethink how we live, come together and talk about it. I think it will be fine.

*Warmth for the Unhoused,
Unfurnished and Uncloseted*
by Pol Esteve Castelló

If David Vilaseca (b. 1964) had not died in a bicycle accident in 2010, I would have probably met him on the dance floor. David was very much part of the LGBTQ+ scene during the years he lived in London from the early 1990s until his death. He frequented gay discotheques throughout his twenties to his forties and recorded his experiences in a series of written reflections which appear dispersed in his two autobiographical novels: *L'Aprenentatge de la Soledat* (*The Learning of Loneliness*) and *El Nen Ferit* (*The Wounded Boy*).[1] To David, the gay discotheque seems to have been an ambivalent space: a source of comfort and frustration, as well as a space of inquiry.

'What do I want from the discotheque? What am I tempted to do there?',[2] a mid-forties David asks himself retrospectively in *El Nen Ferit*.

David Vilaseca was a scholar from Barcelona who specialised in Hispanic queer literature. I am also from Barcelona and an academic, but in the field of architecture. David talks as a Mediterranean man – not too handsome, not too ugly, as he would have probably presented himself – that has migrated to the UK. So do I. The difference is that I arrived in London two decades after him, in 2012, and I experienced the city over a period he didn't get to see. Despite the temporal disjunction, his and my experiences of queer spaces, and particularly of gay discotheques, have many converging points. I say 'gay' to underline that those spaces are and have largely been frequented by homosexual men – although often advertised as queer venues – and 'discotheque' because they normally imply social dancing. Reading David, it feels like the experience of such places haven't changed much in the last three decades. Despite the recent closures of a large number of the LGBTQ+ venues in London, the affects produced on the dance floor still build up on the need to reconsider who is the queered self. With the intention to expand on his inquiry on the power and magnetism of the discotheque, I will navigate his notes, which to a great extend I can subscribe as mine.

When David arrived in London after the most dramatic years of the AIDS crisis, he found a revived night scene. The city was full of LGBTQ+ venues, from colourful cabarets to the dark dungeons. Yet it is the idea of the discotheque that recurrently appears in his writing. Often, he would wake up in the middle of the night with a compulsion to go to a club. He explains this irrepressible desire as a need 'to go out in the search of the Other.' Not a real individual, neither a friend nor a lover, but the kinship of an ideal companionship. Often, though, the desire drifts into a sensory request: 'I want to reproduce that ineffable and infinitely warm sensation I had felt so many times in the past,'[3] he says. The appeal is recurrent, regardless of the type of a club:

> ...firstly the attraction was towards getting into one of the normal Saturday night [discotheques] (...), after a while, what would get me out of bed were the ones that opened in the early hours of the day, finally, around six or seven in the morning, the temptation came from the afterhours. The tempting fantasy was more or less always the same: there I'd find a warm, cosy and akin milieu.[4]

That is also what I want from a club. That is what I miss after not having been able to access the dance floor for a while. I want to reproduce again that indescribable *warm* feeling that I (we) believe to have encountered in the past. Initially, it is presented as a question of temperature: we want the *warmth* back. The reference to comfortable temperature recurs both in casual conversations with friends and writings on the subject of clubs. For example, Amy Roberts – a member of the activist group Friends of the Joiners Arms that won the landmark case against property developers in London and established legal protection for queer space – said about entering the infamously popular, and temporarily disappeared, venue that it 'felt like a warm embrace.'[5]

It seems that we all crave warmth, even if the air-conditioning of a club is blowing at its fullest. But where does the warmth come from? The physical feeling of *warmth* can come from the outside or the inside of the body. In a discotheque, it can be produced by friction – with other bodies – or be an exothermic chemical reaction of your tissues. Or the combination of both. 'The fantasy,' says David, 'is that of the heat of the mist and drugs.'[6] The bodies are overheated by dancing and chatting, internally ignited by ecstasy and libido. In the best world, you are surrounded by a landscape of smooth and moist skin irradiating heat.

In architecture, the relationship between warmth, body and space is commonly linked to the house. Traditionally, the house is spatially and conceptually articulated around a source of physical heat – the fireplace or the kitchen hearth. The warmth that emanates has been seen as indispensable milieu for intimate familial relationships that nurture. Despite Reyner Banham claiming that 'a home is not a house',[7] commonly, the house is understood as the reification of the home. Thus, in a metonymic operation, *home* as the mythical space of comfort and safety is signified by *warmth* – a warmth that transcends the material and evokes the social entanglement provided by the house as the ideal locus of the family. The same linguistic transposition seems to happen in the club. *Warmth* stands for a feeling of *home*.

At one point, David reveals that it is 'in the middle of the dance floor' where he found 'the unequivocal sensation of 'being back' and of 'feeling at home'.[8] I also felt *back home* the first time I entered a gay club in Barcelona and the warmth of the mist caressed my skin. I was *back*, despite having never been there before. It was not that I knew the space or those that were there that night. The feeling was that of an ineffable communality, a form of kinship activated by the kinetic energy of heated particles around me. The feeling of homeliness sprang, even though the discotheque was stripped of any of the elements that traditionally constitute a house. On the dance floor there were no fireplaces, no sofas, no tables, no beds, lamps no windows. But the feeling returned every time I entered a new club in London.

To build a dance floor is to get rid of any prescribed architectural element. When the club occupies an old theatre – as did the former G.A.Y. in the London Soho's Astoria – the chairs from the stalls are literally removed. The dance floor is emptiness; it is a surface indicating space. When the Spanish writer Paul B. Preciado lived in an empty flat in Athens, he experienced the transformative power of an unfurnished space. The bare floor of his living room was like a dance floor: 'the experience is inaugural and aesthetic: a body, a space.'[9] Emptiness is a starting point. Emptiness has the potential to be occupied. Space can be taken in the same way as you can fill a hole in your body. When it starts to fill up, it starts to acquire a meaning. Yet this home cannot be built with bricks and furniture. This empty floor only welcomes bodies; the ones that stripped themselves of the physical and metaphorical architectures that formerly defined them: from the house to the closet.

Over sixty per cent of the LGBTQ+ community in London identify themselves as non-British white.[10] Like David (and me), many left their homes behind – homes understood as both the houses of their families and the countries where they were born. Migration involves a reconfiguration of the past 'through a history of lost homes (unhousings)',[11] says Sara Ahmed. A great number of those that occupy the dance floors, have gone through a process of *unhousing*. We left behind a house and the associated homeliness. In addition, those that transgressed the rules of the binary gender system, went through a process that Preciado calls 'unfurnishing'.[12] His trans body is an *unfurnished* body, it is like 'an empty house':[13] a 'nameless space'[14] that resists any taxonomy. Furthermore, most of those that identify as LGBTQ+, like David, also went through the process of *uncloseting*. As it is commonly referred, we *come out of the closet*, and thus leave the ease of normative life. On the dance floor, cultural and territorial migrations parallel the migrations from the heterosexual and gender-binary regimes. The dancing bodies left behind not only the physical and emotional site of the familiar home of origin but also the security of the future structured around the conventional family's IKEA living room.

The unhoused, unfurnished and uncloseted body is like a Russian doll, from which several material and cultural layers have been removed, leaving the remaining ones to tremble. 'What is doing a professor showing off his butt in a discotheque?'[15] wonders David, implying the inadequacy of a *professor* filling up the dance floor. However, he explains, the dance floor offers the possibility to further remove, at least temporarily, the remaining layers of constructed identity. Using an architectural analogy, one could say you can get rid of the last subjectivating envelopes: of the office, of public transport, of the shop, etc. Above all, one can get rid of the cognitive space of everyday life.

David uses the Deleuzian notion of *deterritorialization*.[16] Operating on a larger scale, above the closet, the furniture and the house, there is the possibility to depart from the territory of the known. When under the influence of the dance floor – the light, the sound, the drugs – he leaves behind this world to enter a place where 'time and space have lost the consistency they normally have.'[17] When entering the club, we leave behind the *phallogocularcentric* regime – as coined by Martin Jay[18] – that mediates our experience of the world. Under the dazzling flashes of the stroboscope and the atomising beams of the laser, the privileged white straight masculine eye has difficulties to see. The beats of the musical rhythm convert sounds into haptic experiences, the reverberation fills up your vowels, and the drugs do the rest. On the dance floor, disposed of any preconceived references, you need to learn to perceive again.

However, says David, the result is not that of losing oneself. On the contrary, on a personal level, *deterritorialization*, rather than eliminating the experience of one's identity, it further accentuates one's own subjectivity:

> This is you more than anyone that you might be in your everyday life. Stripped of all the signs that identify you outside this space, even of the reality that normally surrounds you, thanks to what you have taken, the only thing left of your self at this moment is precisely this: yourself.[19]

Ahmed suggests that when you are at home 'subject and space leak into each other, inhabit each other.'[20] In the home made of bodies joined with a malleable mortar of light and sound, the perceptual patterns of the party intertwine with the bare self. The flash and the blink, the bass and the whisper, the swing and the friction build provisional and tentative architectures to shelter your genuine self. This is at the same time liberating and edifying. Dispossessed bodies peeled to the core gesticulate and essay the postures that will define the architectures and furniture of our future homes.

Yet one needs to be aware that the ephemeral social space of the dance floor is not exempt from struggle. Architecture is an instrument of institutionalisation, and the subtle dynamics of taste, status and coolness that build up in the precarious and corporal architectures of the gay club, often perpetuate existing discriminations or invent new ones. Like any home, the dance floor is not devoid of domestic conflict. But the power of its emptiness to design the self and the homely warmth emanating from this collective work cannot be easily found elsewhere.

Overleaf: Elio Stolz and Ruth Segarra, *Fire*, 2007

This piece is accompanied by the track *Queer Hearing* by John Bingham-Hall. See p.172 for more details.

# *Notes on an Image*
# by Rut Blees Luxemburg

I have always been interested in and drawn to night as a space of freedom. This fascination with the city after nightfall led me to make the photographs that became *London: A Modern Project* in the early 1990s. At the time, together with a group of fellow art students, we ran a gallery on the sixteenth floor of a tower block on the King Square Estate off the City Road in east London. We named the gallery PLUMMET and it quickly established itself amongst other artists and curators, who came to PLUMMET for a programme of exhibitions and events, including a performance sermon by the estate vicar, Father Len.

For me, the high-rise became a production site, an 'out-door studio' where I made works with a 5×4 plate camera. The photograph *Highrise*, of the opposite tower block, Rahere House, was taken for my first exhibition at PLUMMET, as was the photograph *Vertiginous Exhilaration*. When we began installing the exhibition, we were stunned to find out that the framed artwork would not fit into the lift. My friends borrowed some rope from a weekend sailor, and in the nocturnal fog we furtively hoisted the work up to the sixteenth floor on the outside of the building. In hindsight it seems as if the work had to enter the gallery through its own 'birth-canal'.

*Highrise*, in the same way as all the other works in the series *London: A Modern Project,* was taken with a long exposure of over ten minutes, which rendered people who moved in or out of the frame invisible, leaving only their illumination glowing in the dark, suggesting a dynamic, electric energy, *lock down your aerial...*

Left: Rut Blees Luxemburg, *Highrise: A Modern Project*, 1995
Following pages: Rut Blees Luxemburg, Installing *Vertiginous Exhilaration* in PLUMMET, 1995

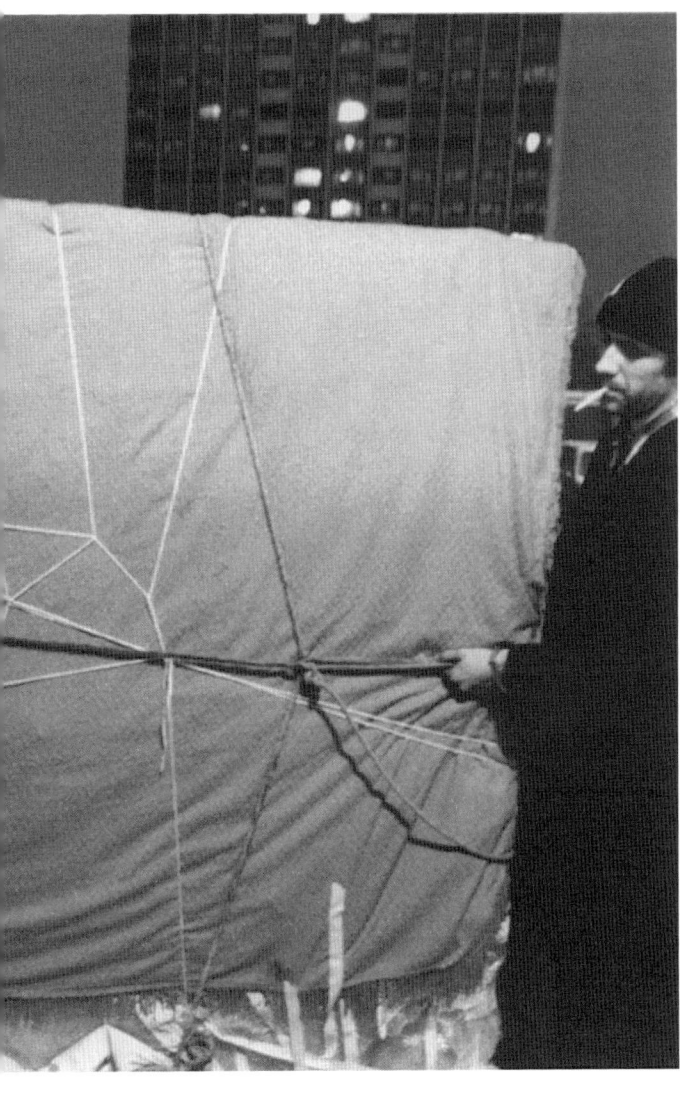

*Scotopia*
by Satu Streatfield

I've always been a night owl. As a teenager I'd have a nap after school and stay up late listening to music. I'd light a single candle in a thick blue glass holder and a violet flame would twitch, sway and vibrate in the dark, setting the whole room into flickering motion, revealing that 'dream world' conjured by the 'wavering light beating the pulse of the night' (Jun'ichirō Tanizaki, *In Praise of Shadows*, 1933).

By the time I got to university, my hours had shifted even further into the night. My interest in the subject I was studying (architecture) waned. The architect Louis Kahn said, 'The sun never knew how great it was until it hit the side of a building'. I preferred to wait for the sun to retire, and the buildings with it. Wandering through nocturnal London, I'd watch its familiar outlines dissolve and metamorphose. I was drawn towards – back towards – the glimmering shadow-light of the ephemeral and its shape-shifting possibilities. And so the clean order, precise lines and unreal gloss of architectural visuals gave way to something more disordered, porous and experimental – charcoal smudges, experiments with the cut-up technique, and images carved out of darkness with light.

Bird's eye
(On flying into London at night)

Swooping down into London at night, the city is Kandinsky electrified, a cacophony drawn in light. Red and white lines trace veins and arteries through the dark countryside. Football pitches are luminous green cards tossed across the land. Pools of sodium light form a string of dull amber beads through suburbia. LEDs paint streets in whitewash and punch holes through the canvas. Repeating grids of bulkheads jut out, each one a social housing block, each point of stark white light signalling a doorway, a home.

Sodium streets
(An ode to sodium light)

Jorge Luis Borges wrote, 'I cannot walk through the suburbs in the solitude of the night without thinking that the night pleases us because it suppresses idle details, just as our memory does.'

I love sodium light. Low pressure (SOX) for its monochromatic, otherworldly orange hue, and high pressure (SON) for its gentle sepia tints. It glows and radiates. It softens edges. Its shadows are rich.

SOX lamps are objects of beauty. Blazing vapour trapped in a glass tube, folded and encapsulated in glass. Glowing wands of amber against a twilight sky, draining the colour from the landscape. A sodium-lit night is a luminous darkness. Sodium recasts everything. It bleeds into surfaces with its chemical hue, rearranges the order of things, flattens and mutes.

My urban night is a high-pressure sodium-lit night. Less otherworldly than its low-pressure counterpart, SON desaturates, renders streets lo-fi. It pours gold into the street, turns foliage bronze. It's a light that shape-shifts and time-travels. It hums forgotten melodies, shows you a faded picture, ignites memory-imagination. It cloaks me in a warm blanket. It feels like home.


Mismatched lamps
(On my secret love of mismatched lamps, colour inconsistency and messiness of urban light)

Architectural lighting designers strive for colour consistency. The LED revolution has seen the terms 'binning' and 'MacAdam Ellipse' all over lighting specs to avoid the tinting or tainting of clean white walls. The lighting designer's eye is tuned to dirty yellows and faint hints of green or pink. Even before LEDs, 'incorrect colour temperature' was a frequent feature on snagging lists.

Perhaps this is why I delight in the sight of mismatched lamps in the city at night. Urban light, like life, is messy, disorderly. I have a particular affection for one stretch of street in my neighbourhood that is lit by three misfit streetlights, each fitted with a different lamp. The street and trees are cast in amber SOX and then golden SON, before crisp, white metal halide unleashes its full palette of colours.

> Bulkhead
> (On one of the simplest forms of lighting – a lamp in a box – and its ubiquitous use in social housing and on construction sites)

This is lighting at its most blunt and utilitarian. A bulkhead light is designed around the shape and size of the lamp, encasing, protecting and displaying it in a translucent, waterproof box. Bulkheads are ubiquitous in social housing and create the nocturnal image of estates all over London. They are the simplest and dumbest way to flood an area indiscriminately with light. The perimeters of estates (and of luxury housing under construction) are lit by this interrogating, bludgeoning light that hinders visibility but screams 'you can be seen'.

Bulkheads also appear in underpasses and construction sites, repeating over and over, in rows and grids, punching rhythms and signals through the urban night.

Apertures and scrims
(On windows and views through their dressings at night)

At night the city turns inside out – the all-seeing, technicolour illumination of daylight retreats, and the hidden life inside buildings is revealed. Curtains and blinds modulate windows at night and turn the domestic into street theatre.

Net curtains turn translucent at sunset. Heavy velvet is a draped silhouette, framing glimpses of domestic life. Cotton glows in smooth gradients of colour, as shadows shift behind.

Fellow night owls and their lit windows are beacons on my way home. A man who lives under a DIY red cove light. Fairy lights dancing through a first-floor bedroom. A living room lit by a single designer lamp shade. A TV bathing a couple and their room in restless light.


In praise of unstable light
(An ode to old fashioned [i.e. not LED] lamps)

The instant, noiseless light of LED is deadening. Give me slow, humming, unstable light that breathes. Give me low-pressure sodium lamps gently warming up, rolling through soft pink to fiery amber against a darkening sky. Give me metal halide lamps and their stuttering start, their buzz and push through meagre green to brilliant white. Give me a dying fluorescent tube, its warm ends glowing and dull vapours swirling, humming and bursting their last pulses of light into the dark. Give me ceramic-dipped silk, mantles whose light fades to a mute warm glow before burning out, gas flames dancing at their edges. Give me the high-pitched rattle of a vibrating, burnt-out tungsten filament. Give me a candle flame wavering, alive in the dark.

Darkness
(On the slow extinction of darkness)

My eyes gasp and my skin prickles when it gets dark. Experiencing true scotopic vision in London is a joy, and is becoming a rarity. Scotopic vision is colourless vision. When I was a child I would lie in bed in the suburban dark, trying to focus on details in my room. They'd float and shift and I'd chase them across the wall until I caught them, suspended them in my peripheral vision. I'd wait, watching them take form, and in an instant they'd disappear.

Now my night time is tinted and animated. The LED indicator lights of electronic devices have crept in. My darkness is the blinking of an internet connection, a mute red light on a TV, two floating blue dots on a sound system.

*Occupying the Shadows*
Interview with ENDGAME
by Andrea Cetrulo

I invited ENDGAME, an electronic music producer, founder of the label Precious Metals and co-founder of club collective Bala Club, to think about ideas of bedroom production and the after-dark. The making, circulation and collective enjoyment of underground electronic music like ENDGAME's, although often brewed in a solitary bedroom, relies on sharing resources and on economies of affect, with the home becoming a civic infrastructure for nocturnal gatherings, staged in communal living spaces such as converted warehouses or mixed-use venues run by their residents.

I came across his music back in 2017, when his album *Consumed* was released. Although I was drawn to the sound in itself, I became intrigued by its broader aesthetics, combining the imagery of gothic horror stories with metallic industrial beats and sinuous Latin and Afro-Caribbean rhythms. It felt like music made for phantoms and nocturnal creatures to dance to. What drives ENDGAME and his community to make music? And, what are the conditions in which it thrives and evolves as an ecosystem?

> AND  Does city architecture and infrastructure inform the imagery of your work? For example, the video for the track *Sniper Redux × Kamixlo*, which you produced, was shot at a council estate in Brixton where a few members of Bala Club live. There is something irreverent about the way you navigate the streets at night from the inside of a neon lit limousine, rapping with your friends on the street and communal staircase while everybody is sleeping. Can you tell us why you chose that site to shoot it and if it is representative of some sort of cosmovision?

END  The cityscape definitely influences the way I approach music and the imagery that goes with it as it's what I know best, it's always at the forefront of my mind when making music. The way music interacts with daily life has always been inspiring for me: hearing tunes through a car window or from someone's phone on a bus. Cities bring music into your life in that way. It's like a constant interaction.

The idea for that video was to contextualise the music we were making, as I felt it could be misunderstood. It needed to be framed. Our approach was left-field in a lot of ways, and we needed to create visuals that went with that: a mix of reality and aspiration. We wanted to make a video that reflected who we are, which at the same time can sit alongside other videos on [grime, rap and hip-hop websites] GRM Daily or WorldStarHipHop.

AND  Both your solo work and your releases with Bala Club feature evocative atmospheres that seem to draw on the after-dark and celebrate it at the same time. The sound and the album artwork aesthetics have a futuristic gothic quality, for example, the allusion to Clive Barker's 1986 cult horror novel *The Hellbound Heart*, which gives the name to a track on your album *Consumed* (2017). Can you tell us a little bit about these references?

END  The music I'm interested in only sounds good at night. Clive Barker is a huge influence. His work is about darkness, not only the darkness within us but also atmospheric darkness. I relate to this a lot. I guess this is part of having a sense of being an outsider, both musically and socially. Occupying the shadows feels more comfortable to me. Barker's work is also about summoning darkness, and I see my music as trying to achieve that, like a portal to the darkest part of you.

Other important references to the nocturnal are: comic books such as Todd McFarlane's *Spawn* (1992 – present) and Grant Morrison's *The Invisibles* (1994 – 2000); David Cronenberg's films such as *Videodrome* (1983) and *Scanners* (1981); the music of artists Tool, Headie One, Vybz Kartel; and fashion designers Raf Simons, Junya Watanabe and FACETASM.

> AND  Would you say your music 'sounds of' the spaces where it's imagined and conceived?

END  My music is an escape from where I'm rather than a reflection of it. I daydream, imagining a world I can inhabit and then go there. My surroundings are never that interesting, honestly, I see my music as escapism.

> AND  Access to recording studios, spaces for hosting parties, and equipment for making videos is not always easy. How did these limitations open up different possibilities for sharing resources with other members of Bala Club and making things happen in a more homemade/DIY way?

END  It's important to be able to make something out of nothing. None of us have any backing or budget for production facilities. The music happens through asking for favours from like-minded people and collaborations that benefit everyone. I think that's a big part of living in a city like London. It's easy to hang out with people from lots of different disciplines and collaborate through an organic process.

In terms of process of making my albums, I compose using a computer software, but I'm not that interested in the technological aspect of it. For me, digital music production is just an accessible tool for self-expression. I don't want it to be defined by the technology I use. If I had a guitar, and felt it were more suitable to what I wanted to do, I would use it.

In terms of working with others, the 'club nights' we organised provided a place for us all to meet. All of the people I am friends with and work with musically really care about music and wear their hearts on their sleeves in that way, which is not something I take for granted. A lot of the music scene is hollow to the core.

AND   Did these dynamics allow those collaborations to flourish, in comparison to the more transient interactions that occur in conventional club settings?

END   I guess the club night we put on didn't function in the conventional sense of what a club is. They were more like meetups or gatherings, a group of like-minded people coming together in a communal setting to share what inspired them or what they were making. It wasn't so much about an audience but each other, and community. Those nights were incubators for ideas.

AND   Can you tell us more about the particular track you chose to include in this publication's sound compilation, and how it contains both the domestic and the nocturnal?

END	The track *TRST RIDDIM* is one from my archive. It's one of my most emotionally charged instrumentals. It's about losing faith but still having hope. It encapsulates that feeling of a lonely journey home on a night bus, when your phone has run out of battery, and you are left with just your thoughts. A sense of self-reflection and tortured melancholy. I try to make work in a way that is true to my feelings and intuition.

ENDGAME contributed the track *TRST RIDDIM* to the audio compilation. See p.172 for more details.

*Darker Night*
by Michael Salu

> Then a new goddam day begins,
> But the sky still is covered up in darkness.
> Let the dark, let the dark
> Last forever,
> Day must not, day must not
> Break at all.
>
> —BERTOLT BRECHT
> *The Rise and Fall of Mahagonny*, 1930

It was during one of the early summer months, but impossible to remember the actual date, restrictions were lifting in Berlin, but like animals kept captive for their safety against the threat of an infestation from an incompatible and incomprehensible species, and released to the wild for the first time, everyone trod cautiously, myself included. Like flitting moths, we evaded each other, and blinked into this new light, wiping crusts from our eyes and fixing the rumples in our oft-worn loungewear. This new light landed differently upon our fallible corpora. This light was less dappled by obstructions – road works, traffic and cranes laying down materials for new multi-floored nests. With less shadows cast, we no longer felt the burn of speed, nor the low fog of hangovers. This new light was more stark and raw – a naked sun. The spectre loomed large like a heavy cloud, its edges fraying as it introduced a storm, yet unseen. Businesses seized the moment, upgrading invisible codebases to entrench our dependence on them.

Time had melted. The formulation of days had grown meaningless, as did – even more so – the distinction between day and night. The effects of lockdown lingered. My *twinned* self was home, increasingly a drifting representation, a crunch of pixels talking with friends captive in their respective tombs nestled in other time zones. Like Phoenician nobles, we surrounded our physical bodies with carefully selected wares to accompany us on into an *afterlife*. The precious gold and minerals so prized by the nobles of yesteryear were now the conductors of technological alchemy enabling us to collectively grieve the previous world. We had the tools to whittle down an endless night into algorithmically tailored monotony and, if we had lowered our blinds or closed our eyes, there would be little difference to discern between, say, my friend's experience in New York, or mine six hours ahead in Berlin.

My twin stayed indoors, partially uploaded. He was intrigued by this need to preserve a fresh sense of selfhood that he had discovered through this extended period of isolation and was, thus far, unwilling to relinquish. The quiet of an endless night. Lamplit explorations of stories. We found the isolation of the writer's life, if not the sometimes-heavy sense of duty that comes with it. My twin represented my desires, and I left him to this fatalistic dance, to walk the streets of the city at night instead. Late, very late. As my footsteps echoed through the hallway to the exit, voices faded and the cackle of black humour of a black moment drifted away like wisps of smoke. I moved away from my twin and the screen's magnetic pull – where the dream world had augmented – and on into the black of night. A city of naked histories whose walls crawled with whispered secrets, now lay dormant, inert. I walked through the desolate Alexanderplatz, the site of so much historical voice, unrest, opinions and pigeon shit, of resistance to the German Democratic Republic, of fireworks unleashed like weapons on each New Year's Eve. All of these historical moments accumulated in the surfaces of this grey expanse and culminated in the Black Lives Matter protests of the summer of 2020.

The night. The wide boulevard of the Karl Marx Allee that so comfortably accommodated Soviet tanks was emptied of vehicles and pedestrians. I walked accompanied only by historical whispers. The windows of the vast and grand frontispiece buildings lining the boulevard – trophy monuments to display the GDR's promise and potential – were only flecked with light, as though the residents of these apartment blocks didn't want to draw attention to themselves. I walked in a solace of silence, for a time–nothing, where the unlit architecture shaded into the dark blue of a moonlit sky. I passed a hotel once popular with young, forty-eight-hour tourists bused in on cheap flights. A glorified hostel, its interior used to scream deafeningly at guests with gaudy signage reminding them to HAVE A GOOD FUCKING TIME in a bold sans-serif font arranged in an acrid yellow against a matt black background. Brand guidelines for the night's revelry. I wondered how the nightlife of a city so historic, providing sanctuary to so many (regardless of one's age or hedonistic predilection) could be put under such semantic control. I saw one of these garish signs through the darkened ground floor windows of the empty foyer as I passed, the words still yelled, but there was no one around to listen – the guests had long since fled. The same fat sans-serif logotype placed atop the hostel's bland modernist structure cut silhouettes into the moonlight. I walked. A souped-up Mercedes thundered past, taking Detroit-conceived techno with it.

The night. This was when they wanted to love you cravenly, almost possess your blood, but during the day they would stare broodingly with distrust. The cover of darkness offered the truth of desire, a fantasy that mirrored the anxiety and scapegoating of the daytime. The night brought down masks; plastic, leather, fabric or latex, and we swirled each other's recently acquired chemicals in our mouths, and switched the responsibilities of real-world for dream-world. At home, my twin, endeavoured to preserve this immediate past, rendering these memories within opaque digital expressions.

Night walks came with an accompanying soundtrack. The light tap of a fox's paws on concrete paving. Sensorial inputs and outputs converged and attempted to straddle other dimensions of comprehension. People gradually filtered out from their homes. Except the night would no longer be the night we dwellers of this city had known. It was something else, but some things remained. The neon of the *Spätkauf* burned out of the ground floor of a row of uniform apartment blocks; a man staggered out parking himself on one of the benches outside. A heartening tradition in Germany placed this furniture outside an off-licence or convenience store to provide a place to make oneself at home for however long a chilled beverage or a personal reflection lasts.

The man had forgotten to open the bottle, went back inside for an opener, before returning to his seat and beginning to roll a cigarette. On this breezeless night, I watched him pause this activity at a midpoint, the tobacco and filter rested on the delicate, open parchment. He stared into space for a long moment, as one might do on a sofa at home, falling into regret or maybe relief behind a stoic face, then he continued.

A Friday evening in mid-August, and this time a date I can remember. A country house in Brandenburg. A Decameron-lite social arrangement for a weekend. An escape. A new shiny barbecue with LED-lit knobs and dials that gave the impression of an extra-terrestrial mothership arriving to offer an exit from this existential rupture. Unfortunately, that evening it could only proffer vegan burgers that bled disappointing simulacra to the charcoaled crust. Their first taste was followed by, well, nothing, when usually it was followed by the meat of meat. Oh well, I did not cry. I enjoy vegan food, just not the simulated kind. Conversations began to flow along with the wine, and I soon antagonised other diners with my observations about culinary mimesis. Berlin, long a home to strong political identity, arguably to the point of rigidity, meant I couldn't help but needle the mirthless way some of the other dinner guests grasped at this valid ethical consideration as something to wear. I felt compelled to aim at their inability to subvert themselves, their prescribed immunisation to irony, or indeed contingency. I watched them resolutely plant their respective flags in the ground, in an almost ritualistic, circular arrangement. *This is where I will stand, the small hill upon which I will perish, the patch of identity upon which I will settle and attempt to grow crops on increasingly arid land and forge my eternal fire,* I could hear them declare within the awkward gaps of conversation that they left me to fill.

A large tea-light candle neared its end on the dining table. A small flame flickered, a small island in a pool of molten, colourless wax. A moth in true kamikaze fashion dived into the hot pool seeking its end, yet seemed overwhelmed by its own commitment to demise. The hot pool welcomed the moth setting one of its wings alight. I watched the moth submerge in its fiery hell, its antennae still aloft and twitching. With the wing aflame, the scene seemed totemic, pagan even. The moth writhed, the sacred flame on its wing undimmed. Suddenly another smaller moth dive-bombed into the fire-water, to its immediate end, or so it appeared. I watched with interest. Its body seemed to float purposefully in the direction of the larger moth, as though the molten pool came with its own sacrificial current to embrace the pioneering moth in immolation. The other moth's flame still burned intensely, flickering in response to my small breaths of wonder at this ode to ending. Except it hadn't ended. I thought there was nothing left to burn, and yet, the wing remained tipped by the undimmed flame, its fuel aplenty.

Bertolt Brecht and Kurt Weil's bawdy satirical opera *The Rise and Fall of Mahagonny* finds three fugitives using the generous cover of the night both to flee the authorities and to set up a 'pleasure city', within which there are no rules, except to enjoy, to consume as much as the stomach and heart can handle. There they aim for the night to never end, yet the night can only be sustained by the activity of the day, or, at least, this is so before time stops, as their pleasure city lies in wait for an imminent hurricane. But the hurricane changes course, and the city is spared, the high-life returns, the night continues. Though as the lead character Jimmy Mahoney discovers when he is sentenced to execution for running out of money before the night ends, capitalism finds a way to inhale everything to reproduce itself, death being no exception.

    Until more recently (at least here in the West), times of war flipped the experience of night and day. The day would leave one exposed and vulnerable. A scurry to find provisions, or a daring child-play outside, could leave one in crosshairs, marked on the viewfinder of a watchful sniper perched on a hill, as an ex-lover from Bosnia once told me about her teenage years in Sarajevo. Night offered more of a chance for survival or military response, depending on which side better knew the terrain.

Friends from Syria and Palestine, noticeably calmer during the events of 2020, talked to me about working during conflict, and how they produced under the prospect of an air raid obliterating where they sat, writing from the gut, often in the dead of night. There was no romance to these retellings, just the urgency of living. A cigarette break upon a roof in Damascus, the sky clear enough to see shooting stars, and below a plume of smoke bleeding up into the night sky from the horizon line of the city. Polish poet Zbigniew Herbert wrote in his poem *Report from the Besieged City*: '...in the evening I like to wander near the outposts of the city along the frontier of our uncertain freedom...'.

I returned home late after walking a loop around the now silent city, sometimes following the faint line of the Berlin Wall. My twin was still up, still hovering above himself, above me, flitting, his body long since compressed and given up to the cold blue glow with an irresistible pull, the enchanting ever-present light amongst the dark.

*Interior Realms:* Audio Compilation

The audio compilation that accompanies this book is a testament to how interior architectural spaces shape music production and how that music, in turn, transforms architecture's atmospheric qualities. The ten tracks invite you to enter ten unknown interior realms: a dimly-lit living room in Skopje in Flora Pitrolo's *Toa e Toa*, a narration of her encounter with Elektro Kultura to the sound of his nocturne *Instrumental*; a house in Glasgow on a languid Sunday afternoon in Cucina Povera's cupboard recording *Aletaan*; a houseboat on the River Lea where, as if performing an animist ritual, Charlotte Law plays guitar to a mineral in *The Stone* (see the prose poem under the same title by Meghana Bisineer and Charlotte Law on page 50); a Dionysian night out at a London warehouse party with John Bingham-Hall in *Queer Hearing* (the audio recording complements Pol Esteve Castelló's essay, see page 134); a journey on a night bus in ENDGAME's track *TRST RIDDIM* (see the interview with ENDGAME on page 156); to the final destination – *Five Rooms at the End of the World*, where Jason Bahbak Mohaghegh reads his essay (see page 78) on nocturnal storytelling to the evocative soundscapes created by William Messenger.

Made in different configurations of domestic space, and without the need for a recording studio or high-end equipment, the compilation strives to embody the spirit of intimacy found in homemade productions intended for consumption in solitary chambers or in the anonymity of the dancefloor after dark.

1. *Instrumental (Toa e Toa version)*
   by Flora Pitrolo & Elektro Kultura

2. *Aletaan*
   by Cucina Povera

3. *The Stone*
   by Charlotte Law

4. *Queer Hearing*
   by John Bingham-Hall

5. *TRST RIDDIM*
   by ENDGAME

6. *Five Rooms at the End of the World*
   by Jason Bahbak Mohaghegh & William Messenger

    6.1  *First Night*
    6.2  *Second Night*
    6.3  *Third Night*
    6.4  *Fourth Night*
    6.5  *Fifth Night*

Released digitally as part of the *Interior Realms* publication.
The compilation can be downloaded from: bit.ly/interiorealms

# Contributors

Alison Irvine
is a novelist and non-fiction writer. Her first novel *This Road is Red* (Luath) was shortlisted for the 2011 Saltire First Book of the Year Award. Her second novel *Cat Step* (Dead Ink), was published in November 2020. She is the writer in the artist collective Recollective and a tutor on the Masters in Creative Writing at the University of Glasgow.

Andrea Cetrulo
is Associate Programme Curator at Theatrum Mundi, and has an affinity for architecture, philosophy, the Atlantic Ocean, and wine. She studied Sociology at the University of Barcelona, and Urban Studies at University College London. She shares her life-long fascination with the occult through her monthly show on Noods, a UK independent radio station.

Casper Laing Ebbensgaard
is Lecturer in Human Geography at University of East Anglia. His research explores the affective and aesthetic politics of the urban night, particularly in relation to urban lighting and high-rise architecture. He recently completed a Leverhulme Early Career Fellowship in which he explored how people inhabit and come to carve out meaningful living spaces in the vertical city at night.

Cecily Chua
is Associate at Theatrum Mundi, where she specialises in research, design, and editorial. She has a background in architecture and her work focuses on the cultural life of our towns and cities, exploring people's lived experiences of their urban environments and the subcultures that evolve from them.

Charlotte Law
is an interdisciplinary artist and musician from Dartmoor, UK, currently based in London, whose sensual, de-creative and durational acts inform a lyrical practice that is led by the landscape. A frequent collaborator, her work incorporates performance, sound, spoken word and moving image. Having performed and exhibited in the UK and internationally, her first solo album *Ice Since Fire* was released by Linear Obsessional in 2020.

Cucina Povera
is a solo project from Finnish-born Luxembourgish vocalist-synthesist Maria Rossi who experiments with layered vocals and found sound. Working in a more studio-based scenario, her work on *Tyyni* (2020) puts emphasis on feelings of distortion and restlessness, and a quiet desire for normalcy. For *The Oystercatcher* (2020), Maria spent a week in the living room of synthesist Ed Simpson in London, where a dark and mysterious modular synth and voice sculpture began to take shape.

ENDGAME
is an electronic music producer, performer, DJ and founder of Precious Metals, a record label and long running NTS radio show. As a co-founder of club collective Bala Club and resident of Endless, his work is embedded in the new wave of club underground music. As of 2021, he is extending the Precious Metals brand to include a record label focused on championing the underrepresented and unknown talents in the hidden corners of the club scene.

Flora Pitrolo
is a cultural critic whose work mostly deals with experimental European music and performance. She works as a writer, lecturer, DJ, and curator. Projects include the archival artist book *Syxty Sorriso & Altre Storie* (Rome: Yard Press, 2017) and the ongoing radio project *A Colder Consciousness* which has been broadcasting on London's Resonance FM since 2011 and on Skopje's Kanal 103 since 2014.

Jason Bahbak Mohaghegh
is a professor and author of comparative literature and philosophy. He has published nine books to date, including *The Chaotic Imagination* (2010); *Inflictions: The Writing of Violence* (2012); *The Radical Unspoken* (2013); *Insurgent, Poet, Mystic, Sectarian* (2014), and his latest volumes titled *Omnicide: Mania, Fatalism, and the Future-In-Delirium* (2019) and *Night: A Philosophy of the After-Dark* (2020).

John Bingham-Hall
is Director of Theatrum Mundi and an independent researcher interested in performances, infrastructures, and technologies of shared life in the city. Since 2015, he has initiated projects with Theatrum Mundi on cultural infrastructure, urban commons, political voice, and sonic urbanism. Alongside this he has collaborated on research projects at LSE and Oxford University, taught at CSM and UCL; published writing across scholarly and arts platforms, and organised queer cultural events (serving drinks whenever needed).

Labeja Kodua Okullu
is a Ghanaian-British writer who lives in London, UK. After studying English and Comparative Literature at Goldsmiths, he went on to complete The Novel Studio writing course at City, University of London and is currently working on his first novel. Labeja has published poetry with *Forward Poetry* and *Rattle* magazine and has essays with *The Smart Set* magazine.

Lyall Hakaraia
is an artist, designer and art director, who has built a community through an arts space VFD that celebrates, embraces and supports *Otherness* in all its diverse forms. Lyall is a founding member of Faggamuffin Block Party and Inter Island, the first Pacific arts collective in Europe.

Marta Michalowska
is a curator, producer, artist and writer based in London. She has recently completed her debut novel *Sketching in Ashes*, supported by Arts Council England through the Developing Your Creative Practice programme, and is currently writing her second one *A Tram to the Beach*, both exploring contested territories. Michalowska is Associate Director of Theatrum Mundi and Director of The Wapping Project.

Meghana Bisineer
is an Indian-born animation artist, curator and educator. She works between London, UK, and Oakland, California. Her practice traverses artist collaborations, experimental film and installation across galleries, art spaces and festivals. Her films have been shown internationally. Since 2016, she has been Assistant Professor of Animation and Graduate Fine Arts at the California College of the Arts, SF, USA.

Michael Salu
is a writer, artist, critic and creative director, whose work and ideas find a place in a multidisciplinary practice. His writing, art and talks have recently centred on where the evolving semantics of technology, language and identity meet. His written work has appeared in many literary journals, magazines and art publications including *Freeman's Journal* and *Catapult*. He runs House of Thought, a creative consultancy and research practice.

Niall Campbell
originally from the Outer Hebrides, has published two collections of poetry. *Moontide* (2014) won the inaugural Edwin Morgan Poetry Award and The Saltire Award for Best First Book. His second collection, *Noctuary* (2019), was shortlisted for the Forward Prize Best Collection. He currently lives in Leeds.

Pol Esteve Castelló
is an architect, researcher and teacher. Their work focuses on the relationship between body, space and technology. They is co-founder of the architecture studio GOIG, is a Studio Master in the Architectural Association and a PhD candidate at The Bartlett, UCL.

RWP
is a published poet and visual artist. She received awards from Creative Scotland and won The Scottish Book Trust Prize for Poetry (2018). She has recently been commissioned by the Scottish Ballet for its 50th Anniversary, The Fruitmarket Gallery, Edinburgh, and the Gallery of Modern Art in Glasgow. She is currently pursuing a PhD at The Royal Conservatoire of Scotland. Her chapbooks *Putty* and *Armatures* were published by Slo-Mo Books.

Rut Blees Luxemburg
is an artist who explores the city and the phenomenon of the luminous. She is reader of urban aesthetics at the Royal College of Art, London where she devised the research project FUTURE ARCHIVE. In 2019 Blees Luxemburg launched the URBAN NIGHT PROJECT with Dr Casper Ebbensgaard, a multi-platform research dedicated to the urban *night*. Her current project *The dark Intestine of Nicolas Ledoux* is a visual exploration of the Saline Royale proto-panopticon.

Satu Streatfield
is a researcher and designer for the urban night. She has worked as a lighting designer since 2006, with projects spanning architecture, art, public realm, events and site-specific, immersive theatre. In both work and play, she explores light and darkness, sound and silence, as media for constructing real and imagined worlds.

Stephen Sutcliffe
is an artist who lives and works in Glasgow. Recent solo exhibitions include Künstlerhaus Stuttgart (2019), Talbot Rice Gallery, Edinburgh, and The Hepworth Wakefield (2017). In 2018 he participated in the Manchester International Festival in collaboration with Graham Eatough on a film for The Whitworth, for which they won the Contemporary Art Society Award. In 2019 he had two books published, *at Fifty* (Sternberg Press) and *Much Obliged* (Book Works).

Victor Ginesta
is a social scientist based in Barcelona. Since finishing his degree in sociology and his MSc in Citizenship and Human Rights (with a specialization in Political Philosophy) he has been working in fields like anthropology, entrepreneurship, solidarity economy, political science, market research or feminist economics. He has also been involved in Barcelona's art scene as a musician, cultural journalist, music selector and underground promoter/curator. He loves languages, cycling and vinyls.

Vladimir Muratovski Divo, aka Elektro Kultura,
is a punk poet and tireless contributor to the Macedonian underground scene for nearly three decades. He recorded the album *Mirovna Poraka* ("Message of Peace") at his home in Skopje in 1992. The record circulated on CD-R until Gjorgji Janevski ran a small reissue of it in 2014 under the label associated with the radio station Kanal 103; it will be released on vinyl on ACC Records in 2021.

William Messenger
is a producer and musician who works primarily with computers through their expressive capacities. His interests include Philosophy, Logic and alternative approaches to Organisation. He studied Philosophy at Birkbeck, University of London.

*Site Report: The Window* by RWP

1  Rainer Maria Rilke, "The Windows", translated by A. Poulin Jr,
   published in *The Complete French Poems*, 2002
2  The name Sharik is taken from the central (canine)
   protagonist in *Heart of a Dog* by Mikhail Bulgakov, 1925

*Collective Matter, Vertical Life* by Casper Laing Ebbensgaard

1  Walter Benjamin, 'Naples', in *Reflections: Essays, Aphorisms, Autobiographical Writings*, ed. by Peter Demetz (New York: Schoken Books), pp.163–73 (p.167)
2  ibid. p.171
3  ibid. p.171
4  ibid. p.172
5  Gaston Bachelard, *The Poetics of Space* (New York: Penguin Books, 1964)

*Into the Night (Or Five Rooms at the End of the World)* by Jason Bahbak Mohaghegh

1  Haruki Murakami, *After Dark* (New York: Vintage, 2008), p.186
2  Jorge Luis Borges, "A History of the Night" in *Poems of the Night* (New York: Penguin, 2010)
3  Griselda Gambaro, "Scene 12" in *Information for Foreigners: Three Plays* (Evanston: Northwestern University Press, 1992)
4  Unica Zurn, *The Man of Jasmine & Other Texts* (London: Atlas Press, 1994), p.25
5  Mahmoud al-Buraikan, "Tale of the Assyrian Statue" in *Modern Arabic Poetry: An Anthology* ed. Salma Khadra Jayussi (New York: Columbia University Press, 1987), p.188
6  Gaston Bachelard, *The Poetics of Reverie* (Boston: Beacon Press, 1971), p.147
7  Maurice Blanchot, *The Space of Literature* (Lincoln: University of Nebraska Press, 1989), p.116
8  Alejandra Pizarnik, "Cornerstone" in *Extracting the Stones of Madness* (New York: New Directions, 2016)
9  Roger Gilbert-Lecomte, "Into the Eyes of Night" in *Black Mirror* (Barrytown: Station Hill Press, 2010), p.89

*In Praise of Reverie* by Andrea Cetrulo & Victor Ginesta

1  Michel Montaigne, *Essais I*, 1580, p.146, online at https://www.cnrtl.fr/definition/rêverie
2  ibid. p.100
3  Gaston Bachelard, *The Poetics of Reverie*, 1971 (Beacon Press)
4  Patrick Leigh Fermor, *A Time to Keep Silence*, 1957 (*The New York Review of Books*, 2007), p.49
5  Charles Baudelaire, "The Double Room" in *Paris Spleen*, 1869 (Alma Classics, 2013), p.9
6  Camille Paglia, "American Decadents" in *Sexual Personae*, (Yale University Press, 1991), p.577
7  Clarice Lispector, "Love" in D*aydream and Drunkenness of a Young Lady* (Penguin Modern: 15, 2015), p.17
8  Charles Baudelaire, "Solitude" in *Paris Spleen*, 1869 (Alma Classics, 2013), p.46
9  Andrei Tarkovsky, *A Message to Young People*. Excerpt from the documentary film *A Poet in the Cinema*, directed by Donatella Baglivo, 1984
10 Richard Sennett, *The Fall of Public Man*, 1977 (Norton, 2017), p.4

11 Kevin Martin, liner notes from CD *Ambient 4: Isolationism*, edited by Virgin in Ambient Series, 1994
12 Oxford Advanced Learner's Dictionary of Current English, Oxford University Press, 2000, p.1095
13 Liner notes from CD *Ambient 4: Isolationism*, edited by Virgin in Ambient Series, 1994

*Warmth for the Unhoused, Unfurnished and Uncloseted* by Pol Esteve Castelló

1 The two novels by David Vilaseca have been published in one single volume in Catalan compiling his complete narrative works: David Vilaseca, *Els Homes i els Dies. Obra Narrativa Completa* (Barcelona: L'Altra Editorial, 2017). The titles of the novels have been translated by the author for reference.
2 David Vilaseca, *Els Homes i els Dies. Obra Narrativa Completa* (Barcelona: L'Altra Editorial, 2017), p.590
3 ibid.
4 ibid.
5 As recorded in Iain Giles, *Trojan Horse / Rainbow Flag* (London: videoclub, 2019), second dialogue page
6 ibid. p.585
7 Reyner Banham famously claimed in a 1965 article published in *Art in America* and titled 'A Home is not a House', that a home is not necessarily composed of the traditional formal elements of the house – from the fireplace to the porch – but that a home can be produced by 'environmental machinery': Reyner Banham, "A Home is not a House", *Art in America*, Volume 2, 1965, pp.70-79.
8 David Vilaseca, *Els Homes i els Dies. Obra Narrativa Completa* (Barcelona: L'Altra Editorial, 2017), p.603
9 Paul B. Preciado, *An Apartment on Uranus* (London: Fitzcarraldo Editions, 2019), p.195
10 Data extracted from: *LGBTQI Nighlife in London from 1986 to the Present* (London: UCL Urban Lab, 2016)
11 Sara Ahmed, "Home and Away: Narratives of Migration and Estrangement", *International Journal of Cultural Studies*, 1999, 2, p.343
12 Paul B. Preciado, *An Apartment on Uranus* (London: Fitzcarraldo Editions, 2019), p.197
13 ibid. p.196
14 ibid.
15 David Vilaseca, *Els Homes i els Dies. Obra Narrativa Completa* (Barcelona: L'Altra Editorial, 2017), p.589
16 David Vilaseca elaborates on Deleuze and Guattrai's notion of *deterritorialization* understood as a form of escapism of the realm of the common sense that defines one's identity in everyday life. His experience of *self-deterritorialization* is accounted in: David Vilaseca, *Els Homes i els Dies. Obra Narrativa Completa* (Barcelona: L'Altra Editorial, 2017), pp.602-604.
17 ibid. p.602
18 Martin Jay explores the concept of *phallogocularcentrism* to describe the totalising effects of the role of vision, in detriment of other senses, in Western patriarchal culture in the ninth chapter of his book: Martin Jay, "Downcast Eyes", *The Denigration of Vision in Twentieth-Century French Thought* (Los Angeles: University of California Press, 1994).
19 David Vilaseca, *Els Homes i els Dies. Obra Narrativa Completa* (Barcelona: L'Altra Editorial, 2017), p.603
20 Sara Ahmed, "Home and Away: Narratives of Migration and Estrangement", *International Journal of Cultural Studies*, 1999, 2, p.341

Theatrum Mundi is a European centre for research and experimentation in the culture of cities with a mission to help to expand the crafts of city-making through collaboration with the arts, developing imaginative responses to shared questions about the staging of urban public life. Based in London and Paris, Theatrum Mundi works through performance, design, publishing, research and teaching with partners across Europe and the Mediterranean.

Theatrum Mundi is a registered charity N° 1174149 in England & Wales and association N° W751251542 in France.

w: theatrum-mundi.org     e: info@theatrum-mundi.org

*Editors*
Andrea Cetrulo and Marta Michalowska

*Audio Compilation Editor*
Andrea Cetrulo

*Contributing Editors*
URBAN NIGHT PROJECT (Rut Blees Luxemburg and Casper Laing Ebbensgaard), John Bingham-Hall

*Cover Image*
Cecily Chua

*Illustrations*
p. 81-93, 171: Cecily Chua

*Design*
Marcos Villalba

*Copy Editing*
Marta Michalowska

*Proofreading*
The Book Edit

*Printing*
Colour Options

© 2021 Theatrum Mundi and individual authors, contributors and rights holders. All rights reserved. No part of this publication may be reproduced, stored in a retrieval system, or transmitted in any form or by any means, electronic, mechanical, photocopying, recording or otherwise, without the prior written permission of the publisher.

Printed and bound in the UK
ISBN 978-1-9161864-3-9